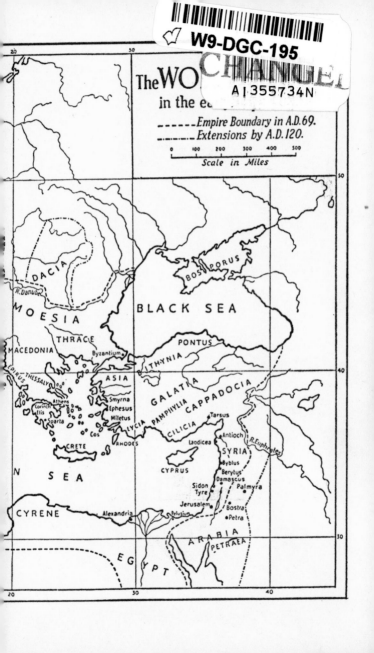

TEACH YOURSELF BOOKS

THE ANCIENT WORLD

This book aims to present an overall picture of the ancient world in terms of its history and peoples. It traces the origin and development of the various civilizations of the Near East, and outlines the growth of the Greek and Roman empires. Emphasis is placed throughout on the cultural and religious backgrounds, and particular reference is made to recent Near Eastern archaeological discoveries and the light they have thrown on the different historical periods. The notes to each chapter, which are listed at the end of the book, refer the reader to works dealing with the subject in greater depth and there is also a select bibliography. For the student and the interested layman, this book provides a concise account of ancient history from the time of the Sumerians to the Christian era.

TEACH YOURSELF BOOKS

THE ANCIENT WORLD

Professor R. *oland* K. Harrison, Ph.D., D.D.

TEACH YOURSELF BOOKS
ST PAUL'S HOUSE   WARWICK LANE   LONDON EC4

First printed 1971

ISBN 0 340 05932 x

Made and Printed in Great Britain
for The English Universities Press Ltd,
by T. & A. Constable Ltd, Hopetoun Street, Edinburgh
Printers to the University of Edinburgh

To

GRAHAM KENNETH

CONTENTS

LIST OF PLATES

PREFACE

The present work is an attempt to portray the outlines of ancient Near Eastern history from the time of the Sumerians until the birth of Jesus Christ.

Some initial space has been devoted to anthropological and archaeological considerations in an effort to demonstrate the primacy of the ancient Near East in the matter of cultural origins.

Subsequent chapters outline the trend of the historical events in antiquity in general rather than in detailed terms so as to present an overall picture of the situation within a comparatively restricted compass.

I wish to acknowledge my gratitude to Mrs. H. Bohne, Librarian of Wycliffe College, for her patient help with source materials, and to the Rev. Norman Green, Assistant Director of the McLaughlin Planetarium, Toronto, for his considerate assistance in correcting the proofs.

R. K. Harrison

Wycliffe College
University of Toronto

CHAPTER I

Prehistory and the Earliest Cultures

The history of the ancient world is now known to be rooted in a prolonged period of prehistory, the exact delineations of which are still far from clear despite a good deal of anthropological and archaeological research. Discoveries of hominid and sub-hominid species in different areas of Africa, the Near East and the Far East have led to a considerable amount of speculation on the part of anthropologists as to the particular areas which could be held to constitute the earliest centres of precivilization. The archaeologists, interested primarily in recovering and examining the remains of man's material past, have had to postulate the origin and diffusion of those attestable cultural elements which anteceded the period when writing was developed as a means of communication.

The difficulties which arise in both fields, however, present serious obstacles to a clear view of the rise and development of human activity in the prehistoric period. Far too much of what has been accepted as fact in anthropological studies is highly subjective and speculative in nature, and depends considerably upon tentative reconstructions from material fragments whose genuineness has often proved debatable among experts in the field. Even when complete skeletal forms have been recovered, it has often been found extremely difficult to date them with a reasonable degree of accuracy.

The problems which arise in this respect in anthropology have not, unfortunately, been lessened by the introduction into archaeological research of such modern scientific techniques as radiocarbon dating. It is now clear that bones contain a minimum of carbon-14 deposits and are therefore unsuitable objects for examination by this method of computation for purposes of arriving at some sort of date for the artefacts.

The progress of archaeological studies has been hampered by the fact that the discipline, which, like anthropology, has only come of age within comparatively recent years, has not been uniformly applied and developed in relation to the particular areas under consideration. Thus, East African archaeology lags far behind that of western Asia. Equally significant is the fact that, while archaeology deals with the consequences of cultural diffusion, it is unable to explain the causes of such activity. Nevertheless, each of these approaches has an extremely important contribution to make towards the objective of setting the ancient world against its correct historic and cultural background.

From the anthropological evidence now available, it would appear that the Pleistocene epoch, which may have commenced about one million years ago, saw the rise of man and the beginnings of human culture. Precisely when or where this began is uncertain, and one of the most spirited debates about physical anthropology has to do with whether *homo sapiens* arose from African or Asian prototypes.[1] Protagonists for an African origin have argued from the presence of such Pleistocene near-human species as *Australopithecus africanus*, discovered at Tauungs in 1925, *Australopithecus transvaalensis* (*Plesianthropus*) and *Paranthropus robustus*, both of which were found in 1936, and the recovery of *Telanthropus capensis* from a cave at Swartkrans near Johannesburg in 1952. However, despite enthusiastic claims to the effect that one or more of the foregoing represent a virtual link between hominid and pre-hominid stock, satisfactory evidence for an African origin of man has yet to be adduced.[2]

Certain euhominid remains have been recovered from eastern Asia, the most celebrated of which, *Pithecanthropus erectus*, was unearthed by an eccentric Dutch doctor in 1891 in the Trinil beds of Central Java. This has been estimated to be between 500,000 and 800,000 years of age. However, it is doubtful whether this species is human, since some anatomists regard it as belonging to an extinct line of large gibbons.

In a nearby locality, von Koenigswald discovered further remains of this species between 1936 and 1939, and these included the brain-case of a child sometimes referred to as *Homo modjokertensis*. The existence of *Sinanthropus pekinensis* was postulated in 1927 on the basis of a single molar tooth, and the species was assigned to the Middle Pleistocene, thus making it contemporary with Java man.[3] The stone tools of the Choukoutien caves also belonged to this period, and are akin to the Anyathian stone industries of Burma, the Patjitanian of Java and the Tampanian of Malaya.

In Europe the early Asian men were matched by such fossils as *Homo heidelbergensis*, found in 1907 and estimated to be about 750,000 years old. Coming closer to the status of *homo sapiens* were two skulls discovered respectively at Ehringsdorf in 1928 and Steinheim in 1933, and dated tentatively at between 150,000 and 120,000 years old. A species thought to be intermediate between Neanderthal man and *homo sapiens* was recovered in skeletal form from the caves of Mount Carmel and the vicinity of Nazareth in Palestine.[4] Dated in the Middle Palaeolithic period, the bones may perhaps indicate that during the Ice Age the inhabitants of parts of the Near East were forced to live in mountain caverns owing to the damp, inclement weather.

Differences in the topographical locations of similar types of fossil species need present no particular problem when it is remembered that during the Palaeolithic period the shape and extent of the land masses in Europe and Asia were quite different in many respects from those which obtain at the present time. Thus, in the early part of the Old Stone Age, Britain was still joined to Europe, the Adriatic was non-existent, the Mediterranean Sea actually consisted of two small lakes and the land masses of Asia were far more consolidated than they are today.

The contribution made by archaeology to the recovery of the earliest material evidences for the origin of civilization in the Near East is very important and may be expected to become increasingly so as investigations are more widely applied to eastern Asia. Braidwood's discoveries at Jarmo in Iraq appear to relate to the transitional phase intervening between food-gathering and food production,[5] while those of Kathleen Kenyon in the lower levels of Jericho have revealed the existence of fully accredited village life which may go back as far as the seventh millennium B.C.[6] Certain traces of the transitional stages of the Mesolithic and Neolithic have been uncovered in northern Iran, and information concerning the nature of the early food-producing village communities has been forthcoming from Egypt, Palestine, Syria and Iran.[7]

If the palaeontologists and archaeologists have interpreted their discoveries correctly, it would seem that the Near East in general and Palestine in particular was a racial melting-pot during the Ice Age, which ended about 10,000 B.C., and that neanthropic man crossed the intercontinental land bridge of Palestine into Europe from what appears to have been his original home to the south-east. Certainly the evidence furnished by the foregoing archaeological sites indicates that the men of the Levalloiso-Mousterian period, who lived on the hill-slopes of the Fertile Crescent, were cave-dwellers for at least a part of every year, and that they included in their diet certain primitive grains and wild ancestors of goats, sheep and cattle.

The first phases of serious agricultural activity in the Near East are usually credited to the Natufians, probably a Mesolithic culture whose Palestinian deposits have caused them to be dated about 8000 B.C. The discovery of a wide range of flint artefacts at Natufian sites has shown that they obtained at least some of their food through the tilling of the soil and the growing of such crops as millet, which they harvested by means of flint sickles and ground to powder in stone mortars.[8]

Somewhat after 8000 B.C., climatic and other considerations made it possible for cave-dwelling to be abandoned in favour of outdoor camps or "proto-villages", which were probably located near perennial springs, as in the case of Jericho.[9] Over the next four millennia there occurred the progressive development of agriculture and the domestication of certain animals. Thus, by 4000 B.C. fully developed village life was in evidence from Egypt to Iran. Important features of this kind of social organization included religious cults with characteristic figurines, mud brick, wattle and daub building, weaving, and pottery-making. The cultivation of grain cereals and some early vegetables, and the full domestication of sheep, goats, pigs and cattle, also took place in the fifth millennium B.C. By 3000 B.C. the prehistoric period came to an end with the rise of civilized society as exemplified by the growth of cities under priest-kings, the development of organized social forms, the beginnings of monumental building, the invention of writing, the growth of mercantile activity and the like.

Despite the claims of both continental Africa and eastern Asia to have witnessed the origin of man, it now appears evident that the earliest centre of precivilization, and of civilization itself, was that area of south-western Asia known as the Near East,[10] from which culture subsequently spread to the remainder of Eurasia. Recent archaeological and anthropological researches have made it clear that, contrary to older opinions, the nations of antiquity were not isolated cultural units who indulged in only the most limited kind of borrowing from earlier or contemporary peoples. Instead, they depended upon their predecessors to a considerable extent, and their own cultures developed out of a complex of traits to which earlier peoples had made important contributions. While this pattern may not have been wholly deliberate, it resulted from centuries of social interaction, and was certainly fundamental to the achievement and diffusion of civilization in the ancient world.

The beginnings of this process can be seen in the Neolithic cultures of northern Mesopotamia, where the period from 6000 to 4500 B.C. is well represented by a number of village settlements, particularly those un-earthed at Nineveh, at Tepe Gawra, some twelve miles north-east of Nineveh, and at Tell Hassuna, a site located somewhat south of modern Mosul. The fact that these villages were all in the same general area suggests that the primitive communities grew up side by side for economic reasons. The lowest levels of the mound at Tepe Gawra yielded pieces of delicately made decorated ceramic ware, some of which was recovered from a burial pit containing Neolithic skeletons. By contrast, the fragmentary wooden huts of the prehistoric period at Nineveh contained broken hand-made pottery of crude design and execution.

In Syria this type of village settlement was represented by the lowest levels of the mound at Tell ej-Judeideh in the plain of Antioch, while at Jericho a pre-pottery phase of the Neolithic has now been well attested.

Neolithic artefacts from Upper Egypt dating as far back as 5000 B.C. have been recovered from village sites identified with the modern settlements of Badari, Deir Tasa and Nagada. The Neolithic culture of northern Mesopotamia and the Assyrian highlands is most probably earlier than the beginning of the fifth millennium B.C., and the nature of the archaeological discoveries to date shows that the people of the New Stone Age were far from being uncivilized.

Palaeolithic sites in Siberia, illustrated chiefly by the middle Yenisei River Valley and the Transbaikal region south of Lake Baikal, show that the western traditions of tool manufacture had spread to the Far East and, if the cultures of the Ordos Desert are part of this movement, to the very borders of China.[11] To what extent these tendencies in Siberia and the Ordos Desert helped in diffusing Palaeolithic culture to China (thereby contributing to the founding of subsequent Chinese civilization) cannot be estimated with any degree of certainty until Upper Palaeolithic sites have been discovered and excavated in China.

A number of eminent sinologists have postulated an extremely long occupation of northern China by Mongoloid types,[12] and have based their views upon the apparent recognition by Weidenreich of Mongoloid features in Peking man and in the species of the Upper Cave at Choukoutien. However, it seems more probable that Hooton was correct in thinking of the latter, at all events, as resembling a primitive European white with some archaic Australoid features similar to those in evidence on the skulls of the modern Ainu of Japan.[13] There do not appear to have been any Mongoloids in southeast Asia at the close of the Ice Age, but after about 8000 B.C. they moved from their place of origin, perhaps in northern Asia, and by the second millennium B.C. had occupied parts of western China and south-east Asia.

This latter area seems to have been an early cultural centre which exchanged influence with India and China, although it has to be admitted that the archaeological picture is not yet sufficiently stable to make possible a proper chronology of these early contributions. A Mesolithic stage (8000-6000 B.C.) seems evident from the discovery of chipped and polished stone axes in south India. These are also found in south-east Asia, whence they extended into China and Siberia.[14]

The techniques underlying such activity most probably came from the early Neolithic period of the Near East, and may only have spread into China after 3000 B.C. The early village farming cultures in Baluchistan date from about 3500 B.C.[15], while the mat-marked and cord-marked pottery of central Asia and northern Eurasia can almost certainly be dated after 3000 B.C. From the evidence to hand it would appear that the earliest cultural influences spread into ancient China from western Asia, and included the early farming of the pre-pottery phase, early village cultures of the Neolithic period, later village society, the use of bronze and the elaboration of painted pottery. South-east Asian influences can most probably be seen in the development of chipped and polished stone tools, the domestication of animals and the expansion of husbandry.[16]

About 4500 B.C. the Chalcolithic or "Copper-stone" period succeeded the Neolithic. With it came the displacement of stone by copper as the principal material for tools and weapons, a development which occurred somewhat before 3000 B.C. The most advanced Near Eastern Chalcolithic cultures have been unearthed in Mesopotamia and Syria, and are represented by occupational deposits of great thickness. The oldest of these, which was widely distributed, was the Halafian, named after Tell Halaf where it was first recognized. The strata exhibited a culture far superior to that of the Neolithic settlements of Assyria, having houses built in a rectangular form on stone foundations and religious shrines constructed on a more circular plan.

The domestic art of weaving had reached a high level at this period and the manufacture of rugs was a well-established practice. The typical Sehna and Ghiordes knots of later Persian carpets were devised at this time, and the same methods of preparation and manufacture of rug materials were employed across the East from Asia Minor to China. To the present day the "Persian" variety of knot is predominant in the basic weaving of Chinese rugs, and this reflects the long history of Mesopotamian influence upon one of the oldest of human crafts.

The beautifully executed painted pottery,[17] which was the most characteristic feature of the Halafian culture, was probably the result of a desire by the potters to match the skills of the rug weavers and basket makers. Roughly contemporary were fresco paintings from the Ghassulian of Palestine and the vase decorations from a site near Persepolis in south-west Iran. The delicate polychrome geometric and floral designs of the Halafian Age were executed with great skill, and remained unsurpassed in beauty during subsequent periods in the ancient East.

The Halafian phase was followed by the earliest clearly defined culture of Babylonia, that at al Ubaid,[18] which also underlay almost all the earliest cities of that region, such as Lagash, Eridu, Ur and Erech. Because of the absence of stone, all houses in these early marsh settlements (c. 3800 B.C.) were made of reeds plastered with mud, or at a later stage from sun-dried mud bricks, and rendered virtually waterproof by a layer of decorative clay mosaics applied to the plastered walls. The end of this period, as illustrated by the corresponding levels at Tepe Gawra, revealed one of the most characteristic elements of Mesopotamian temple construction—the recessed niches, which gave buildings strength and decorative appeal,[19] and made possible the design and erection of the Egyptian pyramids at a later time. Pottery specimens recovered from al Ubaid show considerable stylistic affinities with ceramic ware excavated from the lowest levels of the mound at Susa in Persia. By 3500 B.C. a firm beginning had been made in the development of the irrigation culture which was to be typical of Mesopotamia for the next three millennia.

The Warkan phase followed that of the Obeidian, and this can be paralleled by similar cultural occurrences in Syria and northern Mesopotamia. Writing was coming into increasing use and temples were now constructed on artificial mounds or platforms as a safeguard against inundation. At Uruk[20] traces of the earliest Babylonian *ziggurat* or staged temple were discovered, the building being about 45 yards square and almost 10 yards high. The development of writing at Uruk was apparently preceded by the invention of the stone cylinder seal, a device originally used to identify the possessors of goods or property. The designs on these seals show that, in the last quarter of the fourth millennium B.C., indigenous art had already surpassed anything attained in previous ages.

The Uruk (Warkan) phase continued towards the end of the fourth millennium B.C., and the artefacts recovered from the site of Jemdet Nasr in northern Mesopotamia point to an increasingly complex form of civilization. Bronze was coming into use, while sculpture also made its first appearance about this period in the extreme north of Mesopotamia.[21] The painted pottery at Jemdet Nasr is generally regarded as inferior to that of earlier stages of the Chalcolithic, although writing was more highly developed and more widely used there.

The growth of culture in ancient Egypt lagged behind

that of Mesopotamia, with the Neolithic artefacts from Badari and Deir Tasa being of a decidedly rough character by comparison. Tasian pottery was crudely decorated, poorly shaped and badly fired, and, despite such evidences of an approach to a sedentary economy as grains of ancient cereals and the saddle-querns employed to grind them into flour, most of the food was obtained through hunting or fishing.[22] It was only by about 4000 B.C. that Egyptian Chalcolithic culture assumed a more sophisticated form at Badari, with evidences of grain cultivation, the domestication of animals, and the development of trading relations with the inhabitants of the Sinai Peninsula and the lands to the east.

These advances in culture were implemented by the Amrateans of Upper Egypt, who from 4000 B.C. attempted the systematic cultivation of areas of the Nile Valley. Although they developed certain agricultural techniques and wove flax, in addition to manufacturing a wide array of copper tools and implements, some aspects of their ceramic ware were decidedly inferior to their counterparts in Badarian times.[23]

By 4000 B.C. such civilized arts as weaving, basket-making, the full domestication of sheep, cattle, pigs and goats, the cultivation of grain cereals and some early vegetables, mud brick, daub and wattle building, and the growth of religious cults with characteristic figurine deities formed part of a fully fledged village life which extended across the Near East from Egypt to Iran. About 3500 B.C. the village stage of prehistoric culture had reached Baluchistan and the Indus, though to what extent it penetrated the terrain east of the Indus River is uncertain, despite the ideal nature of some farming localities in the area of the Ganges and elsewhere in the peninsula of India. After 3000 B.C. the cultural tendencies evident in northern and south-eastern Asia also appeared in China.

It will be evident from the foregoing survey that the problem of human origins and the dissemination of culture in the prehistoric period is beset by many unknown factors. What can be stated, however, is that neither topography, politics, racial isolation nor sheer geographical distance were able to prevent the diffusion of concepts and techniques in the period before writing was invented. Very few of the significant advances in culture which arose in eastern and western Asia failed to traverse the continental land masses and reappear in areas far removed from their ostensible place of origin.

Diffusion of ideas, processes or techniques seems to have taken place either by direct transfer from one location to another or by the more gradual method of an exchange of ideas between peoples of neighbouring areas. By whatever means the various cultural developments of antiquity became known, there can be no doubt that the early civilizations were founded in antecedent cultures and depended heavily upon contemporary peoples for their own growth and development. While this process can hardly be regarded as deliberate, since it resulted from the normal trends of social intercourse, it is still true that it was fundamental to the proper achievement of civilization and its dissemination throughout the world.

CHAPTER 2

Ancient Mesopotamian Civilizations

One striking feature of the Chalcolithic settlements of the Near East was that they were almost always located in alluvial areas or river valleys, where irrigation could be employed readily. The Chalcolithic culture has thus rightly been designated an 'irrigation culture", for without this important procedure it would have been impossible for the civilizations of Sumer and Akkad, and the culture of the proto-dynastic Egyptians, to have developed in the manner in which they did.

Pride of place in this matter of civilized advance belongs unquestionably to the Sumerians, a people who entered the marshy delta regions of the Tigris and Euphrates about 3300 B.C. and formed the first historical civilized communities of southern Mesopotamia. They were a swarthy, non-Semitic people of a high intellectual calibre, who may have originated in the Caucasus region or the mountains to the east. They were associated with another neighbouring group, the Elamites, who inhabited the Zagros Mountains and with whom the Sumerians came into early conflict.[1]

With characteristic industry, the Sumerians took over and enlarged the city-state system of the al Ubaid period, and laboured at the task of making irrigation canals in order to drain the land and increase the productivity of the region. Being highly religious, the Sumerians set about formulating theological concepts to meet their emotional and spiritual needs. Their

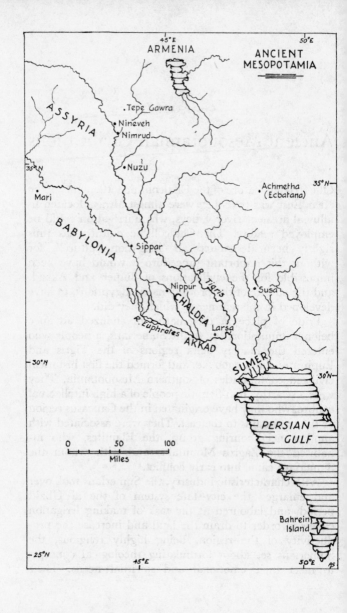

ANCIENT
MESOPOTAMIA

endeavours in this area were so successful that they exercised an enormous influence over the people of the ancient Near East for many centuries. Each community claimed the protection of a particular god, who was venerated as the ruler of a theocratic society, and to him alone was attributed all lordship and authority. During the first half of the third millennium B.C., the Sumerians organized their gods into a pantheon, enlarged the traditions of the cult and built large temples or *ziggurats* as the central feature of each community.

The temples were of more than purely religious significance, for they comprised the focal point from which all community affairs were administered. In the ancient Near East each of the important areas of social organization came under the jurisdiction of the priesthood, and it was this kind of centralized direction that enabled ancient culture to flourish so successfully. Judging from articles found in some temple storerooms,[2] it would seem that craftsmen were active in Sumeria at this time. Silver, gold and copper had all been used in the Uruk phase, and contemporary coppersmiths had devised a means of making an alloy of copper and lead. The Sumerians, however, improved upon Uruk technology by designing new agricultural implements which became popular outside Mesopotamia. They also set their craftsmen to manufacturing a wider variety than hitherto of such ornaments as brooches, pins, ear-rings and toilet sets, and exported some of them to neighbouring countries. They replaced the decorated pottery of the al Ubaid and Uruk phases with vessels which were magnificently executed in bronze, gold and silver, and testified indirectly to the technical skill which underlay their manufacture. In the intellectual sphere the Sumerians made fundamental discoveries in such fields as mathematics, astronomy, medicine and metallurgy, and laid the foundation for successive centuries of usage in astrology, jurisprudence, education, mythology and priestcraft.

The Sumerians must also be accredited with the invention of one of the earliest contributions to art, namely the cylinder seal. This device was made of stone and bore a design in relief which, when rolled across a clay tablet, left a characteristic pattern. Such seals were originally designed to establish individual ownership of goods, hence their use on clay tablets, or across the clay sealing of a jar or some other type of container. The earliest cylinder seals bore designs of such activities as the shepherd protecting his flocks from attack and the king fighting alongside his troops, but later seals became largely formalized and only a very few designs survived. The great popularity of the cylinder seal can be judged from the fact that its usage spread outside Mesopotamia to such countries as Anatolia, Egypt, Cyprus and even Greece.

There can be little doubt, however, that by far the most important contribution which the ancient Sumerians made to civilization was the invention of the wedge-shaped form of writing known as *cuneiform*. It apparently originated as a series of pictographic signs, which were used by the administrative branch of the priesthood for purposes of recording the trading activities, the resources of stock and other functions of the temples. From humble beginnings, the script was modified by successive generations of Sumerian scribes until its pictographic character was replaced by a phonetic or syllabic system of writing suitable for engraving upon clay tablets by means of a reed stylus.

A great many Sumerian tablets have been unearthed by archaeologists at various sites, and on examination have for the most part comprised an amazing collection of administrative, legal, economic and commercial documents which testify to the advanced nature of Sumerian culture. An interesting selection of literary material from Sumerian sites consists of hymns, myths, fables, laments, epic tales and the like, some of which have their counterpart in the writings of the Old Testament. Thus a tablet describing the creation of the sun and moon reads as follows:

"When the gods . . .
Through their unchangeable counsel and mighty
   commands
Fixed the crescent of the moon,
To cause the new moon to shine forth, to create the
   month,
Signs for heaven and earth they fixed.
The new moon, which was created in heaven with
   majesty,
Arose in the midst of the sky . . ."

an account which has some points of contact with Genesis 1: 14-17.

Another notable contribution which the Sumerians made to the growth of culture in antiquity was the development of a system of education. Like all other aspects of ancient professional life, this came under the control of the priestly caste. While the basic aim of the school was to train professional scribes, administrators, government officials and so on, its scope soon became such as to encourage the activities of the *littérateur* and scholar.

Once the beginner had mastered the art of writing cuneiform, he was set to work copying and memorizing lengthy lists of animals, birds, minerals, countries, cities and other material relevant to contemporary life, together with mathematical tables, grammatical texts and glossaries. After this the student copied and imitated the wide variety of poems, hymns, didactic material and other compositions which had become the accepted literary forms over many generations. Students paid

small fees for their tuition and, as with their counterparts in a rather later period of ancient Egyptian history,
were subjected to harsh punishment for misbehaviour.
Most of those who completed their education satisfactorily became temple, palace or government officials,
although there were some who spent the remainder of
their lives in teaching and study.

The enlargement of community life in the early dynastic period brought about the concentration of authority
in the person of a *lugal* or ruler. His office was originally
temporary,[3] but after 3000 B.C. it became hereditary.
So complex was Sumerian society at this time that an
ensi, or executive priest, had to be appointed to organize
the whole of community life in peacetime, and to
mobilize the people and control the disposition of military forces in time of war.

Characteristic of the social life of ancient Sumeria
were the two concepts of law and justice. Economic and
legal reforms were introduced as early as 2500 B.C. to
redress injustices and inequities in social organization,
and these measures served to bring the office of the *ensi*
into greater prominence. While the king or *lugal* was
in theory responsible for seeing that the laws were
observed and that justice was meted out, the actual
mechanics of legal administration were the concern of
the *ensi* and his deputy, the *mashkim*. From the large
numbers of Sumerian legal documents which have been
uncovered by archaeological excavation, it appears that
contracts, deeds, promissory notes, wills and receipts
were the most important matters at issue in the law courts
of Sumer. Of interest also for the history of jurisprudence
is the fact that, by the twenty-first century B.C., some
actual court decisions were being studied in virtue of
having already established legal precedents.

The disposition of individual court cases generally
rested with a tribunal, which consisted of three or four

members of the priestly judiciary. As in modern society, suits could be brought either by the State or by private individuals, with lay or expert witnesses being given the opportunity of testifying as the need arose. Of great importance in the conduct of a trial was the administration of the oath, particularly where witnesses were concerned. Once the decision of the judges had been rendered, it was regarded as legally binding upon all the parties involved in the suit unless fresh evidence came to light which would warrant some significant change in the judgment originally handed down.

Because the concept of democracy is so commonly held to be a product of Greece and specifically of Athenian society, it is interesting to note that the idea of government by representation was fundamental to ancient Sumerian society. The collections of towns and villages of the earlier phases of social development were generally clustered around a larger city, which was governed by a parliamentary structure consisting of two chambers or legislative branches. The more senior of these consisted of what might be described as "senators", while the other comprised younger men who were able to bear arms in time of war.

These two groups were under the leadership of an official who bore the title of "lord" (en). All major decisions connected with the affairs of the city and its satellites had to be referred in a proper democratic manner to these councils, and majority agreement was normally required before the appropriate action was taken. From this early kind of democracy emerged the idea of the king or lugal (literally "big man"), but precisely how this happened is unknown at the time of writing. It may be that the office developed as the result of a further centralization of power in the State or that the concept of kingship was simply borrowed from neighbouring peoples.

Whatever the source, with the rise of the *lugal* there came an increasing degree of rivalry between the temple and the royal palace. In most cities the temple priesthood exercised a good deal of control over the local economy through its huge ownership of land and its employment of skilled craftsmen. As a result, vast amounts of wealth flowed into the temple treasuries from such sources of revenue as rents, interest on loans, and the profits on domestic and foreign trading. This situation presented a threat to the growing influence of the office of *lugal*, but in the end the kings won the struggle by the simple expedient of concentrating all power under the crown through military conquest.

The establishing of dynastic rule in Sumeria about 3000 B.C. seems to have taken place in Kish under a king named Etana. A later cuneiform document described him as "the man who stabilized all the lands", presumably including the territory adjacent to Sumer. Roughly contemporary was the Dynasty of Meskiaggasher at Erech. His son Enmerkar launched an expedition against the distant state of Aratta, probably somewhere west of the Caspian Sea. In antiquity this state was famous for its metallic ores and semi-precious stones. Enmerkar was later succeeded by one of his officers, Lugalbanda, but the Dynasty of Erech became subservient to that of Kish during the rule of the next king, Enmebaraggesi, who defeated the Elamites and established Nippur as the most important cultural and religious centre of Sumeria.

The Dynasty of Ur became prominent at this time under Mesannepadda, whose achievements were reflected in the artefacts recovered from the tombs of the royal cemetery at Ur.[4] Shortly after his death, Erech once again became the capital of Sumeria under the rule of the renowned Gilgamesh. This man became celebrated in song and story, and, although some of his exploits[5]

PLATE 1. An Ivory Carving from Nimrud of the "Woman at the Window". She is probably the goddess Astarte.

PLATE 2. Foundation Tablet of A-anne-padda from a Temple at Ur.
This is one of the oldest extant historical documents.
(*By courtesy of the Trustees of the British Museum.*)

are certainly legendary, Gilgamesh himself was a younger contemporary of Mesannepadda of Ur. The next important Sumerian ruler was Lugalannemundu, who was reputed to have controlled an empire which reached from Iran to the Mediterranean. Towards the middle of the third millennium B.C., Kish became the dominant Sumerian city under Mesilim. By this time, however, the power of Sumer was beginning to wane, and during the rule of Urukagina of Lagash the country was confronted by the threat of conquest from the west and north, by Semitic peoples.

The basic unit of Sumerian society was the family, which seems to have been far more closely knit together by mutual love, respect and the discharge of family obligations than is the case in the modern Western world. Marriage was always arranged by the parents, and the actual ceremony included a contract which was written on a clay tablet. A wife could claim certain important legal rights, such as the ability to hold property, to engage in business and to serve as a witness in the courts of law. Children were under the absolute authority of their parents, but had certain rights of inheritance and were generally the object of much love and affection. The adoption of children on a legal basis was initiated by the Sumerians, and this procedure became a common feature of later Akkadian society, with some variant elements.

Slavery was a recognized institution in Sumeria, despite the fact that most of the inhabitants of the land were free citizens. Some slaves were acquired along with other spoils of war, and on occasions had actually come from a nearby city-state which had been worsted in battle. Others were captives who had been brought from more distant parts of Mesopotamia, while some were freemen who had been reduced to the status of slaves as a punishment for crimes committed against society.

B

Although a slave was regarded as the personal property of his master, he was generally well treated since it was naturally to the advantage of the owner to possess strong, healthy slaves. Slaves could engage in certain types of business activity and could even borrow enough money to secure their freedom at stipulated prices. They were most frequently to be found at work in the palaces, temples and large estates of Sumeria.

Despite the theocratic socialism of the early dynastic period, individuals were able to acquire considerable wealth by means of private enterprise. Some took advantage of the way in which the *ensi* organized foreign trade to obtain a wide range of imported commodities, which they then proceeded to dispose of at a profit. Others dealt successfully in the surplus which existed when their specified quota of goods had been delivered to the temple priesthood. The remains of items imported into Sumeria have been uncovered at Ur, and a little further afield at Mari and Susa, the artefacts concerned including stamp seals of the Indus variety and stone vases from the Bronze Age Kulli cultures of western India. Most of the imported goods, however, comprised the raw materials from which the Sumerian craftsmen manufactured those exquisite products which have come to light through archaeological excavation.[6]

The leader of this movement was Sargon, a renowned military commander and civil administrator, who in the course of half a century conquered most of western Asia and may even have invaded Egypt, Ethiopia and Cyprus. Sargon founded Agade as his capital city, from which came the name Akkad for the more northerly reaches of Sumer, and Akkadians for its Semitic inhabitants. After careful military preparation, he defeated the powerful Lugalzaggesi of Sumeria about 2355 B.C., the beginning of the Old Akkadian period, and occupied the country. He transformed Sumeria into a Semitic realm, consolidated the territories of Sumer and Akkad, and replaced the native tongue with his own Semitic dialect.

These procedures helped the Dynasty of Agade to achieve a kind of political unification which had never been the case previously in Mesopotamia. It was not so much a matter of one strong city-state exercising jurisdiction over another as of the integration of such city-states into a powerful empire. This latter was maintained and even extended by means of a standing army, which was supported by taxes levied by a central bureaucratic system.

The Dynasty flourished in this manner for well over a century, and would doubtless have become a stable political feature of northern Mesopotamian life had not an invasion of Guti mountaineers brought it to an abrupt end. It is unfortunate that, to the present, comparatively little is known of this brilliant phase of Babylonian power as far as actual historical facts are concerned. For this reason it is possible to comment on only the most obvious of the political, economic and social features of the period.

So appreciative was Sargon of Sumerian cultural attainments that he adopted most of them unchanged as the basis of Akkadian life and thought. Excavations at the site of ancient Gasur have testified to the virility of the Old Akkadian period, and tablets which have been recovered have included business accounts and records of commercial transactions which bespoke a highly complex society. Under Naram-Sin, grandson of Sargon, culture reached a new level in Akkad, as is evident from the high degree of artistry exhibited by the Victory Monument of Naram-Sin.[7] But catastrophe overtook Agade in the days of his son, and the growth of the united empire of Sumer and Akkad was abruptly halted by the incursions of the semi-barbaric Guti, who lived in the mountains of Iran.

About 2100 B.C. a fresh cultural upsurge took place in the Sumerian city of Lagash under the pious *ensi* Gudea, who left behind many inscribed statues and other sources of information. The exact scope of his political power is uncertain, but it is known that he had commercial contacts with Anatolia, Egypt, Ethiopia, the Taurus region and probably northern India also. Under Utehegal of Erech the Sumerians broke free from Gutian control and, when Ur-Nammu of Ur gained the political ascendancy, the scene was set for a brilliant revival of Sumerian culture in the magnificent Third Dynasty of Ur (*c.* 2070-1960 B.C.).

The Sumerians returned the compliment proffered by the Agade Dynasty of an earlier day by organizing their administration along the lines initiated by Sargon and his immediate successors. As a result, the political influence of the Third Dynasty of Ur soon extended far beyond the capital city itself. In Elam to the east and Asshur to the north there were provincial governors, particularly towards the end of the Dynasty, whose function it was to ensure that the inhabitants of those regions remained loyal to Ur and paid the taxes imposed upon them by the central administration.

The excavations of Woolley at Ur have given some idea of the splendour and virility of the period. Ur-Nammu, the first king of the Dynasty, adopted the new title of "King of Sumer and Akkad", and instituted a programme of construction and expansion at Ur which made it one of the most magnificent cities in Mesopotamia. Factories and workshops grew up in the area of the temple dedicated to Nanna, the moon deity, and one such establishment was a weaving factory which produced no fewer than twelve varieties of woollen cloth.

Tablets excavated at the site furnished the actual names of the female weavers, the amounts of foodstuffs which comprised their daily rations, the quantity of wool issued to them for weaving and the amount of cloth which they produced. As was the case with other temple-sites in Sumeria and elsewhere in Babylonia, many of the tablets discovered proved to be business documents of various sorts. Prominent among the records unearthed at the *ziggurat* at Ur were ledgers and accounts, the nature of which has thrown a good deal of light on the prosperity which that age enjoyed. At the south-east corner of the *ziggurat* mound at Ur, the excavators discovered the remains of the magnificent mausoleum of the kings who had ruled during the Third Dynasty. It was solidly built of baked mud bricks laid in bitumen and was planned after the manner of a private house. Underground tomb-chambers were situated beneath the floor of the rear of the building and, though the doors of the chambers had been bricked up after the burials, the tombs had been thoroughly plundered in antiquity—a practice which was all too common in dynastic Egypt.

The mausoleum, dating back to about 2600 B.C., was carefully excavated and yielded a wealth of treasures which had an important bearing on Sumerian burial customs and beliefs. Most interesting of all was the discovery that, at that period, Sumerian kings and queens were followed in death by their personal attendants. Dressed in their best robes, these courtiers went in voluntary procession to the burial pit of the dead monarch so as to serve them once again in the world beyond. The cortege which laid to rest the mortal remains of such notables as King Mes-kalam-dug and Queen Pu-abi was apparently led by soldiers dressed in long white robes over knee-length beige tunics, wearing their superb golden helmets and carrying their spears with the points close to the ground. Behind them came the court musicians, dressed in brown robes and carrying the elaborately decorated golden lyres that were common in the early dynastic period of Ur. Then came the grooms

leading the royal ox-carts bearing the body of the deceased monarch, and bringing up the rear were other
ox-carts containing funerary ornaments of gold, silver and
inlaid wood. The female attendants were richly attired
in white robes with red woven decorations along the
edges. Elaborate golden head-dresses were also worn for
the final rites, together with necklets of beads and
colourful links of semi-precious stones.

Once inside the burial pit the procession arranged itself
in proper order, and the oxen were killed and placed
beside the carts. The peaceful sleeping position of the
bodies when found would suggest that the courtiers had
voluntarily taken some kind of sedative or poisonous
drink at that point and had lain down quietly on the
ground before the burial pit was filled in over them.

During the excavations Woolley encountered one
female skeleton which was not marked by a slight
amount of grey powder near the head, which in the case
of the other bodies was all that had survived of a silver
band that was probably used to hold the hair in position.
After looking more closely among the shreds of the
woollen tunic which remained attached to the skeleton,
Woolley uncovered the missing circlet, tightly rolled up
and tucked away in what had obviously been a pocket of
the tunic. In order to account for this unusual situation
he surmised that the female attendant, evidently reluc-
tant to go to her death with her companions, had
postponed her personal preparations until the last
possible moment before the procession began, at which
point she had had no time to put on her silver hairband. If
Woolley is correct in this supposition, this unknown female
is probably the only person in history to have been late
for her own funeral. Abhorrent as the mass death of
attendants may seem, the custom has been attested in
literary texts from Sumeria—as with the story of the
death of Gilgamesh.

Other social institutions of the time, however, were far less forbidding. Marriage was legislated for carefully in the third millennium B.C., and the law-code of Eshnunna imposed severe penalties on any man who married a woman without the formal consent of her parents, the latter being of supreme importance in the absence of a marriage contract. The ceremony itself at this period was both short and modest, except where royalty or nobility were involved, and was chiefly concerned with the formal transfer of the bride from her father's care to that of her husband. The marriage was usually arranged by the parents of the prospective bride and groom, a custom which still obtains in some parts of the world, although love-matches between individuals were by no means unknown. When the father of the bride had received a stipulated bride-price from the family of the bridegroom, the date on which the union would be consummated was set.

As far as the ceremony was concerned, the most important aspect was the sealing of a marriage contract written in cuneiform on a clay tablet. In the presence of witnesses, the father of the bride indicated his readiness to give his daughter into the care of her husband by placing his personal seal on the marriage contract. This was done by rolling a cylinder seal over a specified portion of the contract, and once this was accomplished the marriage came under the protection of the law. The bride and groom were then free to live as husband and wife, and to occupy a place in society as a recognized family unit.

This latter concept was of fundamental importance to the Mesopotamians, who organized social life in terms of the patriarchal system. In such a situation the family was the cohesive force, and membership in it in some form or another was mandatory. Even slaves were included in family membership and as such came under the authority of the patriarch, whether they were directly responsible to him or not. While slaves could obtain their freedom under certain conditions, there was no economic security for them outside a family circle, a situation which naturally discouraged independent activity on their part. Although slaves were not always particularly well treated, the heads of families generally realized that they, too, could well become slaves if their city-state fell to enemy attack, a frequent occurrence during the turbulent history of Sumeria.

Sumerian society reached the height of its development during the splendid Third Dynasty of Ur. Ur-Nammu erected the massive *ziggurat* at Ur which was excavated by Woolley,[8] and introduced a number of social reforms. Sumer continued to prosper under the rule of his son Shulgi, but the land was thereafter threatened by Semitic nomads known as Amurru (the Biblical Amorites), who came in from the Arabian Desert to the west and ultimately conquered such cities as Isin, Larsa and Babylon. In the east, a resurgence of Elamite power ultimately led to the fall of Ur in the days of Ibbi-Sin about 1960 B.C., and this coincided with the Amorite occupation of Akkad under Ishbi-Irra.[9]

A reversion to the old political concept of independent city-states resulted in a revival of Sumerian power in Larsa, with an attendant upsurge of traditional Sumerian culture. Further north, the First Dynasty of Babylon extended the area of the capital city Bab-ilu ("Gate of God") and allied with neighbouring states against an impending Elamite invasion. Power alliances of this kind formed by rival groups of kings in Mesopotamia and Syria were typical of the period between 2000 B.C. and 1700 B.C., as is indicated by the military correspondence recovered from eighteenth century B.C. Mari and elsewhere. The Larsa Dynasty under Rim-Sin made sporadic attacks upon certain allies of Babylon, but this threat to Babylonian supremacy ended with the defeat of Rim-Sin by Hammurabi (*c.* 1792-1750 B.C.), the last great king of the First Babylonian (Amorite) Dynasty.

This brilliant military leader and civil administrator overthrew Elamite power in Sumeria, established his southern headquarters in Larsa, and began the reunification of the north and south. After three decades of rule, he was able to subdue the powerful Amorite stronghold of Mari (Tell Hariri) to the north, thereby establishing the full glory of the Old Babylonian period, which lasted to the middle of the sixteenth century B.C. A number of diplomatic texts recovered in 1933 from the site of Mari included correspondence between Hammurabi and Zimri-Lim, the last king of Mari, and showed that the two rulers had been on good terms for a number of years.

By far the most notable administrative achievement of Hammurabi was his formulation of a uniform legal code for his empire. He collected several earlier Sumerian codes of law, which consisted largely of recorded oral decisions delivered on a rather *ad hoc* basis, and adapted them to the needs of his own day. A copy of this code, inscribed on a six-foot-high black diorite *stele*, was unearthed in 1901 at Susa, where it had been taken by Elamite marauders about 1200 B.C.[10] It depicted Hammurabi standing before Shamash, the sun-god and patron of justice, and the text of the inscription commenced with a prologue which stated that Hammurabi had been commanded by the gods to "make righteousness shine forth in the land, to destroy the wrongdoer and the iniquitous . . . and to illumine the land".

The laws which were then enunciated consisted of about three hundred sections and were stated as having been promulgated in the second year of his rule. The enactments dealt with a wide variety of social, moral, domestic, civil and commercial issues, and were of particular importance because they represented the first major attempt to establish social organization upon a rational and non-magical basis.[11]

Until that time, codes of law had not been brought to the notice of the general public, as they were traditionally regarded as the perquisite of legal officers or priests engaged in study and research. But Hammurabi determined that his law-code would be sufficiently well known by the people to form the basis of behaviour in contemporary society and, accordingly, he erected the *stele* containing the enactments in a courtyard of the *ziggurat* in Babylon, where it could be viewed by interested passers-by without difficulty.

Babylonian society at that time was divided into three groups or classes comprising the patrician or *awilum*, the free artisan or *mushkenum*, and the chattel-slave or *wardum*. When some wrong or injury had been sustained which demanded legal satisfaction, the principle of *lex talionis*, or retaliation in kind, was applied to accommodate the various levels of society according to predetermined scales. Violations of morality were taken very seriously by the Code, and the penalty which it prescribed for adultery was the death of the participants. If, however, a woman was accused of adultery without clear evidence of the offence having actually been committed, she could remove all suspicion either by swearing her innocence or by submitting to the ordeal by water. The latter consisted of leaping into the sacred river and proving her lack of complicity in the alleged crime by remaining afloat.

The Code stipulated that the marriages of contracting parties would only be recognized by law when recorded in writing, and both participants were accorded the right of divorce. A scale of medical fees was prescribed in relationship to the established levels of society, and malpractice was discouraged by means of stern legislation. The construction of houses, rental of cattle, tax collection, river navigation, wage-scales and many other matters of contemporary concern were dealt with in the code, and all these reflected a highly complex background of political and social life.

The *awilum* and *mushkenum* were the two upper groups of society, which corresponded to the patricians and plebeians of Roman times. The third class, which consisted of the chattel-slaves, was as valuable an economic asset for the Babylonians as for the Romans. Slaves were sometimes acquired by capture in times of war, but occasionally they came into servitude as the result of hopeless indebtedness or bankruptcy in their own communities. There were also slave-merchants in all the larger cities of Babylonia, from whom both male and female slaves could be purchased in the open market at prevailing prices.

Particularly desirable for domestic service were the men and women from the mountains to the north and north-east of Babylonia, the districts which in the second millennium B.C. were known as Subartu and Lullu. These hardy mountain peoples were renowned in antiquity for their sturdiness and diligence, and as such they were often mentioned in second millennium B.C. cuneiform letters and business documents. In fact, so widespread was their reputation that the cuneiform symbol for "male slave" is composed of the signs for "male" and "eastern mountains", while a "female slave" is designated by the signs for "woman" and "eastern mountains". Quite obviously, this situation is just about as old as cuneiform writing itself. The cost of purchasing slaves not unnaturally varied from place to place, and also depended to a large extent upon political and economic conditions. The average price was between thirty and forty silver shekels, which usually worked out to something like the cost of three or four ordinary bullocks.

It is interesting to note in passing that the highly proficient porters of modern Baghdad came from an ethnic group known as the Lurs, who originated in the Iranian district of Luristan. This area is adjacent to that which provided the Subarian and Lullu slaves in the third and second millennium B.C. Indeed, it may well be that the Lurs are actually descendants of the ancient Lullu, but conclusive proof of this is lacking at the time of writing. In the period of Hammurabi one of the best known slave markets was to be found at Eshnunna, about twenty miles north-east of modern Baghdad, and located between the hill-country and the larger centres of population to the south.

Slaves were not generally credited with having personalities, but instead were thought of as being items of real property. If a slave was referred to at all in legal documents, it was usually under the designation of "slave unit". If by some chance his name happened to be mentioned, that of his father would be regularly omitted, and if he were injured it would be the master rather than the slave who stood to receive the compensation prescribed by law, since the slave represented a real monetary value to his master.

Some sort of marking was placed upon slaves by the Babylonians, perhaps by means of a branding-iron and possibly upon the hand (one or two cuneiform contracts of sale show that in some cases the owner actually stamped his name on the slave's hand). In addition, a slave wore a small clay tablet around his neck on which was inscribed his own name as well as that of his owner. If a slave ran away, he was pursued by both his master and the civic authorities, and heavy penalties were prescribed in the Code of Hammurabi for those who concealed or otherwise aided runaway slaves.

Female slaves were obliged not merely to give their services to their masters, but also their bodies if he desired coition. Even if a female slave subsequently became a concubine to her master and bore him children, she still remained a slave and could be sold if the occasion warranted it. She and her children could only legally obtain their liberty after the death of her owner.

The most interesting feature of this important institution of Babylonian and Assyrian society was that, despite their complete subservience to their masters under the patriarchal system, slaves were free to engage in commercial transactions, own businesses, have bank accounts and even purchase slaves for their own purposes, such as working smallholdings. Naturally enough, if a master discovered that one of his slaves had considerable business acumen, he had little hesitation in trusting him with important commercial transactions involving large sums of money. However, the more competent the slave, the more equivocal his position actually was, and this situation must have produced a great deal of frustration and friction in ancient Babylonia.

One of the more pressing problems of ancient Babylonian and Assyrian society, and one that seldom receives notice by scholars and historians, was connected with the abuse of alcoholic beverages. The Babylonians made a general distinction between fermented and unfermented drinks, and placed in the latter category the popular palm-tree "wine", which was made by tapping the top of the palm-tree trunk and collecting the sap. When freshly drawn, this liquid was a refreshing and innocuous drink, but it fermented quickly in the heat and after three or four days became extremely potent. A form of beer, which, according to tablets found at Ur, was distributed to certain workers at the rate of a gallon per person, was made by fermenting barley.

Wine was also a popular Mesopotamian drink in the

second millennium B.C., with viticulture perhaps origin-
ating in the Ararat region of north-eastern Mesopotamia
(cf. Genesis 9: 20). Black grapes were mentioned in the
Gilgamesh Epic, and the Code of Hammurabi reflected
the effects of wine drinking upon contemporary society
by regarding the occupation of tavern-keeper as something less than completely respectable. This was a rather
different attitude from that which had obtained in Kish,
a city-state near Babylon, in the Old Akkadian period
(c. 2360-2180 B.C.), where a wealthy dynasty was
established by a certain "Ku-Baba, a barmaid".

Drunkenness was, in fact, an all too common occurrence in ancient Babylonia—and, indeed, throughout the
Near East—and medical opinion generally took the
intoxicating effects of alcohol very seriously, regarding
them as being equivalent to actual poisoning. Thus one
medical text, when prescribing for over-indulgence in
alcoholic beverages, listed the symptoms of the inebriate
in a classic manner: "If a man has drunk too much
strong wine, if his head is confused, if he forgets his words
and his speech becomes blurred, if his thoughts wander
and his eyes are glassy . . .". A perusal of medical texts
from the time of Hammurabi and earlier shows that the
medical profession was concerned about the increase of
personal and social problems caused by drunkenness.

The stability which the rule of Hammurabi brought
to Babylonia encouraged an upsurge of culture in priestly
circles. A remarkable degree of proficiency was achieved
in such scientific fields as botany, medicine and geology,
while extant cuneiform texts dealing with mathematics
and astronomy indicate an acquaintance with a wide
range of mathematical problems.[12] Sumerian religious
traditions were modified to give pride of place to Marduk
as the head of the Babylonian pantheon, and this deity
was made the hero of a lengthy creation epic sometimes
known as *Enuma elish*.[13]

Another celebrated product of the First Babylonian Dynasty was the Epic of Gilgamesh,[14] featuring a king who ruled Uruk early in the third millennium B.C. and whose recorded adventures included an encounter with a devastating flood.[15] The eleventh book of this lengthy epic, which contained the account of the deluge, told how Utnapishtim, keeper of the plant of life for which Gilgamesh was searching, warned the hero that the gods had planned to bring an overwhelming flood upon the city of Shuruppak. Utnapishtim built an ark after the current Mesopotamian pattern and, shortly after it had been completed, an enormous storm raged for six days and nights, flooding the land completely. When the wind and rain ultimately abated, the ark came to rest upon Mount Nisir, and Utnapishtim offered sacrifices to the gods in gratitude for his deliverance. The full form of the narrative in the epic has a number of features in common with the flood described in the Book of Genesis, while at the same time containing a vast number of mythological elements. It is clearly a more highly developed form of a flood tradition which had existed in Sumeria at an earlier period, and very probably depended upon earlier Sumerian liturgical sources.

The only serious rival to Babylonian prestige at this period was the growing might of Assyria under the Amorites, represented in particular by Shamshi-Adad I (c. 1810-1775 B.C.), a contemporary of Hammurabi. Source materials for delineating the beginnings of the Assyrian empire include king-lists, Assyrian eponym lists, and the date-lists of the Old Babylonian period, but they frequently tend to be of limited value in the matter of strict historical information. More useful in this respect are the royal inscriptions dating from such early Sumerian rulers as Mesannepadda of Ur (c. 2750 B.C.), but even these can hardly be considered as direct

historiographic material since they were designed
primarily for the dedication of temples or palaces.

Assyrian history proper can be said to have begun
with a resident *ensi* or governor in Asshur up to about
2025 B.C. After the Third Dynasty of Ur collapsed about
1960 B.C., Asshur became an independent city-state and
the centre of a flourishing commerce, which spread deep
into the Hittite empire of Asia Minor and also into the
mountains to the north and east of Asshur. The Cappa-
docian Texts of Asia Minor recorded the dealings of
Assyrian merchants of that locality in imported textiles,
copper and tin.[16] At this time, trading was established
on the basis of treaties with the native rulers, and the
Assyrian merchants enjoyed a freedom of movement and
a social status which was unparalleled in ancient Near
Eastern history.

Shamshi-Adad I apparently occupied Asshur by force
and at a later time sought to make it the centre of a
territorial state in Upper Mesopotamia. But, although
he was an energetic leader and an enlightened administrator, his regime was no match for that of Hammurabi
and after his death the Assyrian empire crumbled quickly.
His son Ishme-Dagan was able to maintain only military
control over Asshur, and even this prominent city soon
disappeared from the second millennium B.C. historical
scene. With the end of the Amorite empire, various
groups of its citizens moved to the south, and, through
involvement in wars with the Egyptians and Hittites,
became increasingly dispersed throughout Syria and
Palestine, surviving only in the form of small city-states.

This era saw the growth of the Old Hittite empire,
which shortly thereafter engulfed the Fertile Crescent,
swept to the very borders of Babylonia, and brought
chaos and ruin upon Assyria. The Hittites of Asia Minor
were the first Indo-Europeans to penetrate into Armenia
and Cappadocia from the Caucasus region, and during

the third millennium B.C. they intermingled with the indigenous Anatolian Khatti, whose territory they took over and enlarged into city-states. Some of the latter had been first founded when the Assyrian traders flourished in Cappadocia to the east of the Khatti territory during the period when the Assyrians had exercised temporary military control in Upper Mesopotamia (c. 1850-1750 B.C.).

At the beginning of the second millennium B.C., they formed the basis of the Old Empire, which was established in Asia Minor about 1800 B.C. by Pitkhanas, king of Kussar. So vigorous was this culture that for the next two centuries it controlled all the territory from the Black Sea to Syria. Some 10,000 tablets recovered in 1906 by Winckler from Boghazköy in east-central Asia Minor have provided striking testimony to the nature and influence of this mighty empire. The site of modern Boghazköy was that of Hattusas, which for four centuries (c. 1600-1200 B.C.) had been the capital of the Hittites, and the tablets which were found there included the royal archives of the Hittite empire.

The official cuneiform Hittite was only one of several languages in use in the realm, and some of the others are still incompletely deciphered. Legal codes recovered from Hattusas have been found to contain laws parallel to secular prescriptions in the codes of Hammurabi and Moses, and were remarkable in antiquity for their humanitarian emphasis.[17] Hittite religion was of a highly syncretistic nature, and included elements from Sumer, Akkad, Assyria and Egypt.

From the diversity of local cultic practices, the Hittite priests constructed an official pantheon, one member of which, the sun-goddess Arinna, became the supreme patron of the state and the monarchy. The "husband" of this deity was the weather-god Hatti, whose cult became widespread through ancient Anatolia. Propitiatory offerings were brought to him by the temple priests, and animals were sacrificed to secure his personal blessing and promote the fertility of the land.

Occasional instances of human sacrifice have been found in the cuneiform texts recovered from Boghazköy, and in each case they only appear to have been offered under very pressing circumstances. Religious festivals included a spring rite for reinvigorating the earth, and a ceremony held at the vernal equinox in which the king himself not infrequently took part. As in Mesopotamia, magic and divination occupied an important place in day-to-day living.

The religious shrines of the Hittites varied from a comparatively simple type of open-air sanctuary to the elaborate Cyclopean structures which were found at Boghazköy. The latter followed the Babylonian pattern, in which a number of small rooms were grouped around a central paved court. The principal difference lay in the fact that, whereas the Babylonian inner shrine was connected directly with the courtyard, thus enabling the worshippers to obtain an unimpeded view of the religious proceedings, the Hittite holy place was approached by an indirect route. This latter would suggest that deliberate restrictions were imposed upon the numbers of worshippers allowed in the inner shrine, which may, in fact, have only been patronized by the royal family and the priestly hierarchies.

The Hittites made important technological discoveries relating to the smelting and manufacture of iron for commercial purposes and, until the collapse of their empire about 1200 B.C., they monopolized this important area of commerce. In addition, they were renowned horsemen, and claimed the distinction of having introduced the horse and the iron-fitted horse-drawn chariot to the Near Eastern military scene, thereby revolutionizing earlier methods of warfare.[18]

The movement of the Indo-European Hittites into ancient Anatolia coincided roughly with the entrance of the Hurrians into Upper Mesopotamia from an Indo-Iranian source. These non-Semitic peoples flourished from the middle of the third millennium B.C. to the end of the second millennium B.C. and, because of migratory movements, were scattered throughout the Near East. They were well established in Canaan by the time of the Hebrew patriarch Abraham, and in the Old Testament historical writings they were known variously as Horites, Hivites and Jebusites.

During the Hebrew Patriarchal Age (c. 1980-1700 B.C.), the Hurrians were occupied in consolidating their hold upon northern Mesopotamia and by the fifteenth century B.C. were in firm control of a flourishing domain with the city of Nuzu as its capital. The site of the latter was excavated by Chiera from 1925, and from the thousands of clay tablets recovered from the family archives of several villas in the city it is now possible to reconstruct the political, social and religious background of the period with remarkable accuracy.[19]

One legal tablet from Nuzu (Yorgan Tepe) described the activities of a mayor of the city who had been in office about 1500 B.C. and had used his public position to indulge in immoral behaviour, accept bribes and employ workers allotted to public projects for his own purposes; he had also associated closely with a band of kidnappers. Finally, the outraged citizenry could tolerate his behaviour no longer, and he was arrested and brought to trial for his misdeeds.

Most of the Nuzu texts, however, consisted of private or family documents, and often dealt in some way or other with the matter of adoption. Whereas the Sumerians had had the welfare of the child at heart in instituting adoption procedures, the people of Nuzu employed them as a legal device in order to cover up the transfer of land

and estates. According to Nuzu law, the land was in reality the property of the gods and, as such, could neither be bought nor sold legally by its human tenants, who were regarded as holding it in trust for the gods. However, when an individual was adopted, he was expected as part of the procedure to bring along a "filial gift" for the privilege of acquiring the estate belonging to the adopting couple, and in this manner real property changed hands for valuable considerations without actually being sold in the ordinary sense. Along with this subterfuge, however, there were genuine adoptions, undertaken by childless couples with a view to perpetuating their name and removing the opprobrium imposed upon the family by the fact of childlessness. Most adoption contracts contained a clause to the effect that, if a natural son were born to the couple after the adoption, he would take precedence in the family as the real heir of the adopting parents.

The position of the firstborn was of great importance in ancient Semitic society for it usually involved, amongst other things, the receipt of a double portion of the estate on the death of the parents. Local customs permitted the "birthright", or title to the rights of the firstborn, to be negotiable under certain circumstances among members of the same family. One tablet from Nuzu recorded the transfer of inheritance rights to an adopted brother, while another contained the agreement by which a man named Tupkitilla turned over his rights of primogeniture in exchange for three sheep. This procedure goes far towards explaining the circumstances lying behind the familiar Biblical story involving the transfer of the birthright from Esau to Jacob (Genesis 25: 31-33).

The greatest political accomplishment of the Hurrians was the establishing of the Mitanni empire, with its centre in the area dominated by Harran in the middle Euphrates valley. At its height, during the second millennium B.C., the Mitanni empire dominated Assyria for two centuries, and stretched from Alalakh in the west to Arrapkha and Nuzu in the east, maintaining a balance of power between the Hittites and the Egyptians. Even more important than their political activity, however, was the cultural influence of the Hurrians. Already, in the time of Hammurabi, they had composed religious texts in their own tongue, which, curiously enough, had no generic affinities with other Mesopotamian languages, and some of these tablets were recovered from archives at Mari. Hurrian texts of a few centuries later were found at Boghazköy and Ugarit, and there are abundant indications of Hurrian cultural influences in the laws, religion, art, literature and vocabulary of their ancient Hittite neighbours.[20]

One other racial group who were prominent in the second millennium B.C. should be noticed at this juncture. They were an element of Mesopotamian society known as the Habiru, who arose about 2050 B.C. The Habiru were not primarily a race, for they included Semitic and non-Semitic stock, and were probably nomads originally. They were first mentioned in Sumerian texts from the Third Dynasty of Ur, and from then on were referred to in cuneiform texts from every important archive in the Near East. According to the Nuzu tablets, they often hired themselves out as slaves, either to wealthy households or to government officials. On other occasions they were depicted in texts as aggressive, migratory groups, preying upon small settlements and ambushing caravans travelling along lonely trading routes. Some of them were craftsmen and musicians, while others gradually abandoned their nomadic way of life and settled down in urban centres. Some Habiru had west Semitic names, some had Akkadian, and there were a number who had non-Semitic names. From the lists at Boghazköy, the Habiru would seem to have been some kind of social

group of a lower order, occupying a position between
the free citizens and the slaves. On the other hand, texts
from Alalakh and Tell el-Amarna appear to have thought
of the Habiru as a separate ethnic group. Quite possibly
the term "Habiru", which is probably the Akkadian
ḫabiru or *ḫapiru*, may originally have been an appellation
which later developed into an ethnic term.[21]

By about 2000 B.C. Mesopotamian civilization had
penetrated eastwards as far as the Indus valley to
supersede the early village stage which had existed there
for well over 1,000 years before that time. Settlements
of the pre-Harappan variety have yet to be found in any
significant extent east of the Indus, despite the suitability
of some of the terrain for that kind of occupation. As the
evidence now stands, the Indus civilization appears to
have come into being in its full form without demon-
strable antecedents and, unless future archaeological
discoveries in northern Baluchistan, Afghanistan and the
north-west frontier area furnish decisive indications to
the contrary, it must be concluded that Mesopotamian
civilization was antecedent to that of India, although
each naturally produced its individualized cultural
forms.

Excavations at the mounds of Harappa and Mohenjo-
daro,[22] the first of which is the type-site of the Indus
civilization, uncovered traces of an earlier village culture
upon which the citadel had been erected. An advanced
degree of social development, which can be assigned
with confidence to approximately 2500 B.C., was indicated by the co-ordinated planning evident in the design
of the citadel. The technological achievements of the
Harappians were demonstrated by the presence of
sixteen furnaces at the site, together with a crucible
used for melting bronze.

A group of granaries discovered at the northern end
of the mound had been arranged symmetrically in two

rows of six, separated by a central passage and constructed in such a manner as to occupy an area of approximately 1,000 square yards. Barrack-like quarters for workmen were not unlike their Egyptian counterparts at Ezion-geber, Gizeh and Deir el Medineh, although they were by no means as isolated. Evidence of attempts at town-planning were also uncovered at Mohenjo-daro, another major location of the ancient Indus civilization situated in the Larkana district of Sind. Although the mound had suffered seriously from erosion, the excavations of 1928 uncovered some important areas of the citadel, including the community granary and an assembly hall, as well as a complex of buildings which may have been used by city officials. The streets of ancient Mohenjo-daro were laid out in a grid-iron pattern enclosing rectangular blocks of land of approximately equal size, an arrangement which was more advanced than similar attempts at town-planning in Babylonia during the reign of Hammurabi. The walls of the houses were constructed almost entirely of baked brick, although, as was the case in parts of Mesopotamia, sun-dried mud brick was used principally for the interior walls.

These and similar ancient sites, such as Chanhu-daro and Sutkagēn-dor, show that the Indus civilization acquired its impetus from a combination of trading and agricultural pursuits. Harappan sites point to the abundant use of copper, bronze and tin in the manufacture of domestic utensils, tools and weapons of war. Copper may have been imported either from Afghanistan or southern India, and perhaps tin was also obtained from the former area.

Fragments of a camel skeleton unearthed at Mohenjo-daro suggest that the species had been domesticated at an early stage and was already being used as a beast of burden, a view which is supported by the representation of a seated camel found on a bronze rod in a second millennium B.C. grave at Khurab in south-east Persia. This evidence also accords with similar steps taken in Mesopotamia and elsewhere before the second millennium B.C. to domesticate the camel and employ it as a means of transport. Thus, when Parrot was excavating Mari he discovered camel bones in the ruins of a house belonging to the pre-Sargonic era (*c.* 2400 B.C.), while an eighteenth century B.C. cuneiform text from Alalakh in northern Syria contained a list of fodder for domesticated animals in which the camel was specifically mentioned. At Harappan sites archaeologists also unearthed terra-cotta models of solid two-wheeled and four-wheeled ox-carts.

The culture of the Harappan variety appears to have flourished until the sixteenth century B.C., after which it became decadent and proved unable to cope with the initial Aryan invasion of the Punjab and its environs. Excavations at Mohenjo-daro have borne mute testimony to the violence which accompanied the fall of the citadel and have furnished a general date of 1500 B.C. for the end of the ancient Indus civilization.

The foundations of Chinese culture are difficult to locate in one specific area. Traditionally, the Chinese homeland has been regarded in terms of such provinces in northern China as Shansi, Shantung, Honan, Kiangsu and Hopei, in the plain of the lower Yellow River. However, it may well be that some sites in the river valleys of Kansu province in western China, as well as in the general area of the Szechwan basin in the southwest, also made important contributions to the growth of Chinese civilization in ancient times.

Other influences were disseminated from western Asia, and apparently included farming, early village cultures and subsequent village organization, the latter coinciding with the use of bronze for agricultural implements, tools and weapons of war. From south-east Asia, after 3000 B.C., came the impetus for manufacturing chipped and polished stone tools, the use of crops such as rice, the domestication of the water buffalo and, after 1200 B.C., the technique of manufacturing silk.

A prehistoric site near the modern village of Yang-Shao in the province of Honan was discovered in 1921 and found to contain some excellent examples of painted pottery, as well as mat-marked bowls and pedestal stands. Stone tools recovered from the site included spear and arrow points, axes, hoes, adzes and knives. The bones of pigs, dogs, goats and sheep were also found there, along with some grains of domestic rice.

The painted pottery tradition of Yang-Shao was perpetuated at sites in the Ho-Yin district, as well as in the Feng River Valley west of Honan.[23] Early skeletal material recovered from the North China Plain shows that the inhabitants were Mongoloids who were very little different in character from the present occupants of the Yellow River basin. The nature of the painted pottery culture exhibited at the foregoing sites is such as to imply that it stands rather late when compared with the chronology of its counterparts in western Asia.

CHAPTER 3

Palestine and Egypt

The upper reaches of the Tigris and Euphrates witnessed a great many migratory movements at the beginning of the second millennium B.C., not the least important of which was the westward thrust of a Semitic group known as the Arameans. Although traditionally regarded as descendants of the Biblical Shem[1] or Nahor,[2] their tribal name seems to have been a geographical designation which was applied by the Assyrians to a nomadic tribe from the land of Arame, a locality in the foothills of Armenia in north-eastern Syria.

The Arameans had already penetrated as far as Egypt before the second millennium B.C. by following the ancient trading-routes, and they were officially mentioned in Egyptian records as early as 3100 B.C. Other groups moved eastward and settled ultimately in Lower Babylonia, where about 2700 B.C. they were described in Akkadian tablets by the name *Sutû*. The Arameans also seem to have continued the culture of the Amorites of Mari, whose territory they occupied after the time of Ishme-Dagan, and this fact accounts for the reference to the Arameans as a political group in the Amorite texts from Mari, and also in the tablets from Ras Shamra (Ugarit).

Aramean power was concentrated in the area of land between the Habor and Balikh rivers, two great tributaries of the Euphrates. Here there were a great many small city-states which were so powerful that they

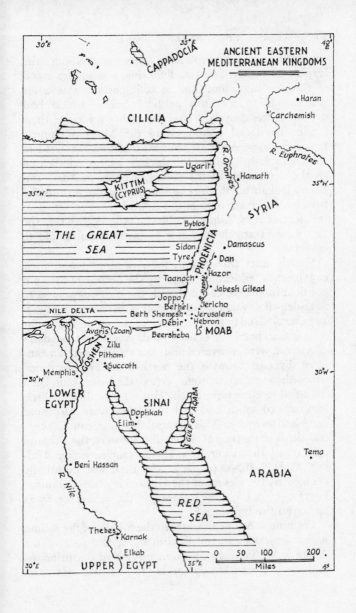

ANCIENT EASTERN MEDITERRANEAN KINGDOMS

extended Aramean influence westward along the
Euphrates to Carchemish, following a common trend
of Semitic migration. The most important reason for
this expansion was the political eclipse which had
overtaken the Assyrians after the incorporation of their
former territorial holdings into the Mitanni empire.
However, some Assyrian political tradition managed to
survive in Asshur during this dark period, as is indicated
by the occurrence of the names of Shamshi-Adad and
Ishme-Dagan on three occasions in the three centuries
between the death of Shamshi-Adad I (c. 1775 B.C.) and
the accession of Ashur-Uballit I (1365-1330 B.C.), the
first king of any importance to bring renewed life to
Assyria.

Shortly after this period, the Arameans found their
expansionist tendencies halted by the decline of Mitanni
political influence, coupled with the vigorous policies of
Arik-den-ili (1319-1308 B.C.) and Adad-nirari I (1307-
1275 B.C.). Under these two rulers the territories as far
west as Carchemish, lost since the days of Shamshi-Adad I
of Assyria, were recovered and, as a result, the Arameans
were diverted towards the north-west. The displaced
tribes then settled in some areas which had not been
occupied to any extent by the Hittites, and little by little
they moved south and east until they were very near
Assyrian territory. This reversal in Aramean fortunes
was the consequence of the conflict between the Mitanni
rulers and the rising New Hittite empire under Tud-
haliyas II (1460-1440 B.C.). The issue was eventually
decided by the victory of the Hittite king Suppiluliumas
(1375-1335 B.C.), which brought the whole of Syria
under Hittite influence.[3]

Prominent Aramean states in the middle of the second
millennium B.C. included Sam'al, at the foot of the
Amanus Mountains; Gurgum, on one of the principal
highways from Mesopotamia to Cilicia; Hamath,

located between Aleppo and Damascus; and Zobah, lying north of Damascus in the metal-rich anti-Lebanon mountains. By the time of the Hebrew Judges (*c.* 1225-1020 B.C.), there was a strong concentration of Arameans near the sources of the River Jordan. One or two small states were also located east of the Sea of Galilee along the western border of the land of Bashan. Most of these groups were internally weak, and their chief strength seems to have lain in their ability to engage in short-term military or political alliances when confronted by some threat to their security.

Their expansion into Syria brought home to the Hittites the danger of a resurgent Assyria, and in the fifteenth and fourteenth centuries B.C., the period covered by the celebrated Tell el-Amarna tablets of ancient Egyptian origin, they endeavoured to enter into an alliance with Babylonia. Assyria was also aware of the latent hostility of Babylonia, and this led to the first conquest of Babylon under Tukulti-Ninurta I (1244-1208 B.C.), who carried off the statue of Marduk, the patron deity of the city. At the same time as they were engaged in reducing the opposition of the Babylonians, the Assyrians were also being encouraged by the Egyptians to curb Hittite territorial expansion.

The Egyptians had for many centuries exerted an important military and political influence upon Palestine and Syria. The expansion of community life in the Egyptian pre-dynastic period (*c.* 4500-2900 B.C.) was continued in the proto-dynastic phase (*c.* 2900-2700 B.C.) of the prehistoric period, and blossomed into the characteristic culture of ancient Egypt in the Old Kingdom period (2700-2200 B.C.).

The late prehistoric period saw the development of agriculture based upon an irrigation economy. Fields were laid out in square plots near the irrigation canals, from which water was transferred by breaching the small

dykes which separated the squares. The rich black soil
of the Nile Valley was tilled by both men and women
using wooden mattocks, and it produced abundant
quantities of barley, emmer-wheat, millet and oats,
together with such vegetables as beans. Hunting was an
important means of supplementing the supplies of food
at this period, and the quarry included lions from the
desert areas, and the more edible animals and birds
from the regions of the papyrus marshes and swamps.
Pre-dynastic hunters wore tattoo marks on their arms and
legs, a practice which may have been introduced from
Libya. They also attached a wolf's tail to the back of
their short hunting kilts in the belief that it would confer
on them the strength, cunning and swiftness of that
animal.

Excavations at proto-dynastic sites have shown that
the hunters used long curved bows of the African type,
and pointed their reed arrows with sharp, chisel-shaped
tips of stone. They also used fine curved flint knives, a
double-bladed axe of hard stone, a boomerang made of
wood, a mace with a pear-shaped stone head and a
lassoo made from palm-fibre rope. For hunting game the
pre-dynastic Egyptians used a large, slender, black dog
of a breed which is now extinct, but which resembled a
greyhound in proportions.

In the Old Kingdom and later periods, netting wild-
fowl in the marshes and papyrus swamps was both a
sport and a means of livelihood, the chief attraction
being the wild goose, the pintail duck and the widgeon,
all of which were in plentiful supply during the migratory
seasons. The usual method of catching the birds involved
the use of a hinged net spread out beside a baited pool.
When sufficient birds had gathered at the spot, the trap
was sprung by the four or five fowlers usually present.
This was done in such a way as to knock the birds on
their backs and trap them under the net. Those birds

which did not manage to get away were promptly put into wooden crates by small boys and used either for food or for restocking poultry farms. Sometimes whole families would go out for a day's hunting in the marshes, and on these occasions it was not unusual for household cats to be taken along too so that they could act as retrievers for injured game which had dropped in inaccessible places in the marshes.

Farmers in the Old Kingdom period had managed to improve somewhat upon the agricultural techniques of the proto-dynastic phase, particularly in the use of the plough, which was drawn by teams of long-horned African cows. In other respects, however, they were very conservative by nature and lacking in inventiveness, with the result that they continued to employ the crude agricultural machinery of their remote ancestors. Even in the highly important matter of irrigation, the old and laborious method of dipping water by hand from main channels to smaller ones continued until about the fifteenth century B.C., when it was replaced by the well-sweep. This latter was a Mesopotamian invention, consisting of a weighted pole balanced on a wooden stump or similar base, and linked by means of a rod to a shallow container which transferred the water in small quantities from a well to an irrigation ditch.

An important place in the social and educational systems of the Old Kingdom and subsequent periods was occupied by the professional scribe. A highly skilled vocation which was rewarded handsomely, it demanded a thorough knowledge of the language, literature and history of Egypt, as well as an ability to communicate in various forms of cuneiform writing. In addition, the Egyptian scribe was expected to be proficient in such matters as law, mathematics, accountancy and general administrative procedures—and even mechanics, surveying and architectural design. Once a scribe had become properly qualified, he was exempted from menial labour and could rise through regulated stages to the very highest offices of the civil service.

Life was undoubtedly very pleasant for the upper classes in ancient Egypt. The country estates of the Old and Middle Kingdom periods were surrounded by orchards and walled parks, which were in the care of professional gardeners. Pools containing lotus flowers, water-lilies and other aquatic plants were to be found on every estate. These, however, were intended for orna-mental purposes—not for bathing. The flowers and shrubs included jasmine, cornflowers, oleanders, man-drakes and dwarf chrysanthemums, while sycomore figs and date palms were to be found in every orchard. A retinue of household servants and slaves attended to all domestic matters, leaving the owner of the estate and his family to enjoy a variety of leisure pursuits.

The middle classes also managed to lead comfortable lives, even though they could never hope to match the affluence of the nobility and the royal family. A middle-class civil servant in the Middle or New Kingdom periods would own his own house and probably a small acreage of farmland outside the town or city. While the furnishings of his home would be modest, they would be of good quality, with some of the more prized articles being imported from countries in the Near East or the Aegean. Out of their day-to-day living expenses, the family would be able to save sufficient money to send a son to the scribal school at Thebes and thus assure him of a profitable future.

The peasants in Egypt, then as now, were invariably at the bottom of the economic scale. They worked hard all their lives at the level of bare subsistence and, as can well be imagined, were frequently negligent and in-efficient in their tasks. They lived under the poorest of housing conditions, and their meagre diet consisted

PLATE 3. Mesopotamian Cylinder Seals. The impressions, produced in relief on moist clay, show various mythological creatures and deities.

(*From the Wycliffe College collection, by courtesy of the Principal.*)

PLATE 4. An Assyrian King, probably Sargon II, in conference with one of his Officers (right). This relief was recovered from Khorsabad.
(*By courtesy of the Trustees of the British Museum.*)

principally of onions, coarse wheat bread, some vegetables such as beans, the figs from sycomore trees, and
whatever could be acquired as the result of hunting and
fishing. Nutritional diseases were all too common, and
infant mortality was appallingly high—amounting to
about 90 per cent. of all live births, according to one esti-
mate. The artisans were generally in a better position in
ancient Egyptian society, but they, too, had to work hard
for their living and were beaten without compunction if
they appeared to be slack, inefficient or incompetent.
As their culture amply testifies, the Egyptians placed a
high price on craftsmanship, and when their own people
were unable to supply specific demands they were not
averse to importing people from other nations to meet
their needs.

Of the skilled workers, the stonemasons were probably
the most valuable, since their constructional activities
were prominent in all periods of Egyptian history. In
the Old Kingdom, stonemasons were in great demand
for the building of the various pyramids which served
as funerary monuments for certain royal personages.
The drawing of plans for these structures was in itself
a vast undertaking which occupied several years. Once
this had been accomplished and the site selected and
surveyed, it was possible for the great blocks of limestone
needed in the construction to be brought from the
quarries, a difficult and dangerous task for which slave
labour was often used. The blocks were generally dressed
at the site of the future pyramid by stonemasons, who used
heavy bronze chisels for the purpose. The huge stones
were moved around on wooden platforms to which
rockers had been fitted, or on a wooden base which
passed over rollers; but, despite these mechanical aids,
they were still bulky and cumbersome objects which
exacted a continuous toll on the workers in terms of
injuries and deaths. A great deal of technical skill went

C

into the building of a pyramid. Most of the instruments used were crude in nature and it is a remarkable testimony to the abilities of the ancient Egyptians that, through their precise surveying, a structure such as that of Khufu is almost perfectly oriented in terms of the compass.

This pyramid, the largest of the Old Kingdom funerary monuments, was constructed in the Fourth Dynasty by its founder (Cheops) at Giza. The work of planning began almost as soon as Khufu had ascended the throne, and from the start it was meant to be the largest and most magnificent ever likely to be erected. When the site had been chosen and quarters for the workmen built, the thirty-year task of construction commenced. The first decade of this period was taken up with the exacting task of measuring and carving from the solid rock a 13-acre foundation for the pyramid, as well as in the building of a ramp-like causeway over 400 yards long up which the huge blocks of stone could be hauled from an especially prepared landing wharf. About 2700 B.C. a force of 100,000 workmen began the construction of the pyramid itself. They were given free clothing and lodgings, but their rations of food were scanty and seem to have consisted largely of onions. Water-carriers were always present at the site to alleviate the thirst of the workers toiling under the hot sun, and Egyptian doctors were also on hand to treat illnesses and injuries. For nearly two decades each July, when the River Nile was in flood, great blocks of limestone, already excavated from the Mokktan Hills just eastward across the Nile, were floated to the site on barges and other craft to join the huge piles of grey and red sandstone, diorite and alabaster which had been brought from the quarries of Aswan, 500 miles up the Nile, and from other locations. When, about 2680 B.C., the highly polished granite cap was set in place on the top of the structure and the scaffolding was removed, the pharaoh and his hierarchy assembled for a ceremony of dedication to mark the completion of the prodigious task. It is estimated that the finished pyramid contained 2,300,000 stone blocks weighing an average of $2\frac{1}{2}$ tons each, making for a gross weight of some 5,700,000 tons. Some of these stone blocks weighed as much as 60 tons each, and were placed on a layer of cement no thicker than a sheet of writing paper.

Some of the granite work on the inside of the Great Pyramid was so carefully tooled and polished that a thin knife-blade could not be inserted between the joints. The royal burial chamber, the very core of the grand pyramid design, was made entirely of highly polished red granite, the ceiling slabs of which would alone weigh about 400 tons. Quite obviously, the feats of craftsmanship and engineering involved in the construction of this magnificent edifice[4] were as much a monument to the skill and abilities of its designers in this remote period of history as to the memory of Khufu, who commissioned it. Unfortunately, in later ages the surface of the pyramid was defaced in part by builders, who found it more convenient to remove the surface limestone than to quarry their own stone, and this had the unfortunate effect of lowering the height of the pyramid from 481 feet to about 450 feet.

The Second Pyramid of Khafre, the brother of and successor to Cheops, stood on a slight rise of ground some 500 feet south-west of the Great Pyramid and was so constructed that the diagonals of both pyramids were in a straight line. The cubic area of this edifice was about 60,000 cubic feet of rock which weighed about 5,310,000 tons (this pyramid was also pillaged in later times by builders who removed some of the facing-stone). The Third Pyramid, built by the son of and successor to Khafre, occupied only about half the area of the Great

Pyramid, but it is nevertheless considered by many to be the most magnificent of the three major pyramids at Giza.

Another important cultural advance which occurred in the Old Kingdom period was the development of the absolute lordship of the pharaoh. He thus became venerated as a descendant of the gods and therefore as the supreme mortal in the land. Next in authority to the divine king came the vizier or "prime minister" and under him were the heads of the various administrative branches, such as the treasury, the judiciary, the diplomatic service, agriculture and so on. Initially, these high offices were monopolized by members of the royal household, but as time went on the nobility became increasingly prominent in the more responsible areas of military and civil administration.

By the time of the Fourth Dynasty, hieroglyphic writing had been developed to the point where it met all the normal needs of government, business and religious circles. Painting, statuary and relief sculpture also attained high levels at this period, and depicted the various classes of Egyptian society in characteristically detailed and well-organized fashion. In the Fifth Dynasty it became customary for inscriptions to be written on inner walls of the pyramids, and these texts dealt with the themes of judgment and final felicity, both of which were matters of incessant concern to the ancient Egyptians. These "Pyramid Texts"[5] are therefore very important sources of knowledge concerning Egyptian morality and religious beliefs.

Unlike their Hebrew counterparts, the ancient Egyptians had always believed in a continuity of life after death. While it is impossible to say just how far back this belief went, there seems little doubt that the elaborate funerary customs evident from the Old Kingdom period onwards were prompted by it. In order to ensure a valid continuity of physical existence after death, the practice of mummification, which was perhaps originally the prerogative of Egyptian royalty, became widely used by the upper and middle classes. Behind this procedure was the thought that the body was the dead man himself enjoying a perpetuation of physical existence in the tomb.

Religious ceremonies attended the preserving of the corpse and were carried out by an appropriate branch of the priesthood. According to Herodotus (*Hist.* II, 86), the brain was extracted piecemeal through the nostrils by means of an iron hook, after which the cranium was rinsed out with wine and resins. Then the abdomen was incised and eviscerated, leaving the heart intact, and again the cavity was rinsed, after which it was filled with myrrh and spices. The corpse was then soaked in a solution of natron for a period of time, which varied from thirty to fifty days depending upon the final cost of the funeral. At the end of this phase, the body was removed from the solution and wrapped in long strips of fine linen. The mummy was then covered with a coating of resin, which served to hold the linen in position and exclude the air completely. Just before the funeral the body was placed in a coffin, which was frequently painted on the outside with a representation of the deceased individual. Sometimes the inside of the coffin was elaborately decorated with pictures and hieroglyphic texts, the latter consisting of magical spells placed within easy reach of the dead person should he need to use them at any given moment. From the Middle Kingdom onwards these "Coffin Texts", as they are called, were written on papyrus and placed beside the deceased in the coffin. At the funeral, four Canopic jars containing the viscera of the corpse were placed alongside the body in the tomb, at which time the personality of the deceased individual was thought to return to his physical frame.

The Pyramid Texts indicate that, in the minds of the ancient Egyptians, the souls of the departed ascended to the sky-goddess Nut and could be seen at night in the form of stars shining on her celestial body. One consequence of this belief was that the burial chambers of the tombs and the coffins themselves were transformed from being merely the houses of the deceased into miniature representations of the universe. The ceilings of the burial chambers were adorned with stars, while the inside of the coffin lids generally bore some sort of picture of Nut. Where inscriptions occurred on the outsides of coffins, they invariably included a welcoming greeting from the sky-goddess to the deceased.

From an early period, the followers of the sun-god Re believed that human life very closely paralleled the course of the sun. Just as life began and terminated, reflecting the transition from morning to evening, so the analogy required that death should not be final and that there should be a rebirth on another morning. Thus it was imagined that when a man died he went to the west, called "ŏnkh" or "life" in Egyptian, the locale where both the deceased and the sun went in order to "have a rest in life", as the Pyramid Texts of the Fifth and Sixth Dynasties phrased it.

Overshadowing Egyptian daily life was the thought of the judgment which a man had to face immediately after death if he aspired towards resurrection and renewed life. It was accordingly believed that, on his decease, a person came face to face with Osiris, the supreme ruler of the dead, to have his heart weighed in the balances. The *Book of the Dead*, a haphazard collection of ancient magical spells and practices relating to life after death, described the way in which the judgment took place in the presence of Osiris and his forty-two assessors. On a balance set up before the god, the dead man's heart was weighed against Truth (*ma'at*) and, if the weighing was satisfactory, the deceased was entitled to life in the kingdom of Osiris. If unsatisfactory, the unfortunate person was thrown to the "devourer of the dead"—a monstrous combination of a crocodile, lion and hippopotamus—which was stationed beside the balance. Precisely what it was which determined how the balances would act was never made explicit in Egyptian literature, but there can be little doubt that a high degree of moral behaviour in life would ensure a happy existence for the individual beyond the grave.

Ancient Egyptian religion was characterized by a large number of gods, an astonishing range of cultic objects and the consistent worship of sacred animals. The latter is frequently described as totemism; but in point of fact this is an incorrect designation, since the typical features of totemism, such as the claim of descent from the totem, its sacrifice for purposes of ceremonial feasting among members of the clan and the prescriptions relating to exogamy, cannot be found in Egyptian sources.

The pre-dynastic period saw the rise of two cults which were more widespread and distinctive than their contemporaries. One of these was the cult of Re, located at Heliopolis, a city quite near to Memphis. Re was the all-powerful sun-deity, who was believed to have originated in the waters of the Underworld, and was self-created. In turn, he gave rise to other cosmic deities, including such notable gods of the Egyptian pantheon as Isis, Osiris, Set and Nephthys.

By the end of the proto-dynastic period the cult of Re had won a great many adherents, and shortly thereafter its doctrines began to proclaim that pharaoh was the offspring of Re, or even the great deity himself in incarnate form. Elaborate cultic rituals were devised in which the pharaoh was involved in a daily representation of purification rites thought to be associated with the functions of the sun.

The other ancient cult was that of the deity Thoth, son of the falcon-god Horus, and this was most prominent in Hermopolis, a city in the Nile Delta. An ibis on a raised standard formed the cultic emblem of Thoth, and this god was believed by his followers to have created the world, brought the forces of nature under control and bestowed culture upon the human race. Thoth was the god of wisdom and, as such, was supposed to act in the Underworld as the scribe who recorded the divine judgments when individual spiritual values were being assessed by Re after death.

About the time of Menes of Thinis (c. 2900 B.C.) another religious cult arose, this time in Memphis. It acknowledged Ptah as the supreme god and was unusual in that its doctrines were of a decidedly intellectual nature, a situation which stood in marked contrast to the crudities of the other cults. Ptah was venerated as the great cosmic Mind, the First Cause, who had produced the world and its contents by the projection of his thought.

Despite the existence of the foregoing cults, it must not be supposed that ancient Egyptian religion was ever a unitary whole, since there were always a number of deities who were worshipped independently in various localities. The nearest approach to a national religion came with the cult of Osiris, Isis and Horus, but this only became widespread after the Middle Kingdom period. Other deities claimed their own theological systems and, although they were sometimes identified with various gods of superior stature, they were never either amalgamated or reconciled. At best, they existed side by side with the principal gods in a complementary manner, thus making for an extremely confused situation on occasions.

The decentralization of the State which had commenced in the Fifth Dynasty continued into the Sixth

Dynasty (*c.* 2350-2250 B.C.). Tomb inscriptions make clear the increasingly prominent place which provincial nobles and officials were occupying in the governing of the kingdom. This situation was due in part to a greater emphasis upon friendly relations with foreign nations, and to the expansion of trade and commerce which resulted from such a policy. Local antagonism was sometimes encountered, however, and during this period the Egyptians sent no fewer than five expeditions against the people of southern Palestine and one seaborne attack against the inhabitants of the north Carmel region.

With the end of the Sixth Dynasty the splendour of the Old Kingdom period waned, and the Seventh Dynasty introduced a time of social upheaval which is generally known as the First Intermediate period (*c.* 2250-2000 B.C.). The lack of a strong centralized government contributed most of all to this phase of instability, which also saw the infiltration of Asiatic Bedouins into the Nile Delta region. The Seventh and Eighth Dynasties exercised a weak rule from the region of Memphis, but the two succeeding dynasties arose in the vicinity of modern Cairo. Perhaps the inadequacies of Old Kingdom materialism led to an interest in the cult of Amon-Re of Thebes, a deity who was held to constitute a unity of spirit and matter.

About 2100 B.C. the struggle for power in Egypt narrowed to a contest between Memphis and Thebes, and when the latter emerged victorious about 2050 B.C. the way was opened for a reunification of the country. This was achieved under Amenemhet I, the founder of the Twelfth Dynasty, who instituted the second great age of Egyptian history known as the Middle Kingdom period (2000-1780 B.C.). Social organization was renewed along feudalistic lines, Nubia was conquered and brought under Egyptian control, trade was established with Phoenicia and northern Syria, and Palestine again fell under the cultural domination of Egypt. The Twelfth Dynasty was particularly noted for the development of the Sinai copper mines, and for the improvement of trading relations between Egypt and the Semitic nomads of Palestine and Arabia.

The Middle Kingdom period saw a good deal of religious consolidation, in which many local deities were subordinated to the all-powerful god Re, the sun-deity. Another popular development was the worship of Osiris, in which the myths concerning the suffering, death and resurrection of this god were perpetuated in ritual form. To the century following 1850 B.C. belongs that curious collection of material known as the "Execration Texts". These documents consisted of magical formulae for the cursing and defeat of pharaoh's enemies, which were inscribed upon pottery and subsequently smashed in a special ceremony. Superstitious though these sources were, they nevertheless pointed to the existence of opposition to pharaoh both at home and abroad. This situation crystallized into political upheaval, and the resultant strife between a weakened rule at Thebes and a competing dynasty in the Nile Delta brought about the end of the Middle Kingdom in approximately 1780 B.C.

Two successive dynasties were unable to maintain Egyptian frontiers intact, and about 1700 B.C. the Hyksos poured into Egypt, using the compound Asiatic bow and the iron-fitted horse-drawn chariot originated by the Hittites to make their victory complete. The Hyksos were of mixed Semitic-Asiatic stock, and may even have included some Habiru.[6] They established their new capital at Tanis about 1700 B.C., and from this strategic location in the Nile Delta they began reorganizing Egyptian social life and expanding commercial relations with neighbouring countries. They accepted tribute from a weakened dynasty at Thebes, but ultimately the latter acquired Hyksos weapons and rebelled against the hated invaders about 1580 B.C.

Unfortunately, the period of the Hyksos rule in Egypt is one of considerable obscurity, due chiefly to the lack of Egyptian historical inscriptions during this time of conquest. The fact that the Hyksos were most careful to observe Egyptian conventions, even to the point where they simply took over the bureaucratic administration already in existence, did not endear them in the least to the conquered native populace. As time passed and the Hyksos appointed naturalized Semitic officials to high administrative offices, the bitterness of the Egyptians increased and they began earnest preparations for the day when the invaders would no longer be supreme in the land.

An Eighteenth Dynasty ruler named Sekenenre was killed in an early attempt to drive out the Hyksos, but the fight for freedom was carried on by his sons Khamosis and Ahmosis I. The latter launched an attack against Tanis, and when it fell to repeated blows the Egyptians from the south made a concerted effort to expel the Hyksos, an objective which was achieved when the invaders were finally driven from the Nile Delta region about 1570 B.C. The fugitives retreated to Hyksos strongholds in southern Canaan, but after a siege of some three years they were forced to surrender. Egyptian forces then occupied the remainder of the old Hyksos empire in Syria and Palestine, and thereafter only the occasional Egyptian raid into Canaan was necessary to maintain order there.

The general background of Hyksos rule makes it quite legitimate to assume that large numbers of Israelites were in Egypt at this time, in accordance with the traditions in Genesis 47: 27, and that they remained behind in the Delta region after the Middle Kingdom had come to an end about 1780 B.C. It is probable that some aspects of the work of Joseph survived from the latter end of the Second Intermediate period (1780-1570 B.C.), which included the rule of the Hyksos in Egypt. This may be seen from the fact that when the invaders were finally expelled, the land, with the exception of temple property, belonged to the pharaoh, as it had done on a previous occasion when Joseph organized the country to meet the perils of famine, as recorded in Genesis 47: 20-26.

The shock of foreign domination for so lengthy a period made the Egyptians resolve that such a situation would never occur again, and as time went on this feeling of imperialistic patriotism increased. Under Ahmosis I of Thebes, the founder of the Eighteenth Dynasty, the New Kingdom period commenced (c. 1570-1150 B.C.), and without any question its brilliance was inspired by a desire on the part of the Egyptians to blot out the unhappy past and make the future more splendid than ever. As a result, there was a dramatic resurgence of activity in the fields of architecture, literature and art. Profiting from their tribulations at Hyksos hands, the Egyptians reorganized their armed forces and became proficient in the use of the chariot and the compound bow. The old feudalism of the Twelfth Dynasty was replaced by a dictatorship, and at the beginning of the New Kingdom period the ordinary Egyptians found themselves no better than serfs who were required to cultivate the land for the benefit of its royal owner.

When Ahmosis I died about 1546 B.C., he was succeeded by his son Amenhotep I, who reigned until about 1526 B.C. A year or so later Thotmes I, the son-in-law of Ahmosis I, came to the throne and established firm military control over the Egyptian provinces of Syria and Canaan. The daughter of Thotmes I was Hatshepsut, a woman of strong personality and outstanding organizing ability. In compliance with the matriarchate, a

social system by which inheritance passed through the
female rather than the male of the family line, the son
and successor of Thotmes I, who happened to be the
half-brother of Hatshepsut, married the queen and thus
became the pharaoh Thotmes II. This man died a few
years after one of his concubines had borne him a son,
Thotmes III, and while this youth nominally shared the
rule of Egypt with Hatshepsut it was the latter who really
decided policy in Egypt. It was not very long before
she seized power, adopted the title of "king"—much to
the surprise of the populace—and wore the double crown
of Upper and Lower Egypt. For some eighteen years
(c. 1486-1468 B.C.), she ruled with vigour and expanded
Egyptian influence abroad by her ambitious commercial
enterprises. Her mortuary temple at Thebes devoted a
great deal of space to depicting her trading expedition
to the land of Punt, at the southern end of the Red Sea,
whence she brought back incense, spices, gold, apes and
ebony.

Within a few months of the death of Hatshepsut,
Thotmes III (1490-1436 B.C.) set out on a military
campaign against the inhabitants of Palestine, an event
which would seem to imply that the peaceful policies of
Hatshepsut had now come to an end. In a subsequent
campaign Thotmes III, who was a renowned warrior
and an able commander, defeated a coalition of Canaanite and Hyksos forces at Megiddo about 1480 B.C.[7]
Although he spent the next eighteen years in building up
a large Near Eastern empire which extended as far as
the Euphrates, Thotmes III was careful to develop the
internal strength of Egypt also, with the result that by
the time of his death the land had attained new heights
of imperial stature.[8]

Thotmes III was succeeded about 1436 B.C. by his son
Amenhotep II (c. 1436-1422 B.C.), a powerful and valiant
noble who waged two successful military campaigns in

Syria. One of these was directed against a Mitanni prince who seems to have been inciting local rulers to rebel against the Egyptians. Large numbers of prisoners were brought back as slaves, and the group included over 3,000 Habiru. The successor of Amenhotep was Thotmes IV (c. 1422-1398 B.C.), who renewed diplomatic relations with Asia by marrying a Mitanni princess. A mural of this period, from a tomb at Thebes, portrayed the arrival of a group of Syrians bringing tribute to the royal court. [9]

Amenhotep III succeeded to the throne of Egypt about 1398 B.C., and ruled until about 1361 B.C. During his reign the enlightened Eighteenth Dynasty reached its height in a massive expression of cultural attainment. Ostentation became particularly noticeable as the wealth of the land increased, and this trend was reflected in the grandiose nature and elaborate decor of the temples of that period. Artistic representation was profoundly affected as a result and, because Cretan influence predominated over that of Asia Minor, Africa and Mesopotamia in this field, the art of the Egyptians became livelier and more naturalistic in expression. Sculpture in the round replaced the familiar bas-reliefs of earlier dynasties, and the new artistic concepts issued in such products as the celebrated bust of Nefertiti, wife of Amenhotep IV, which represented the highest level of artistic execution ever attained by the ancient Egyptians.

Amenhotep IV (c. 1369-1346 B.C.) broke with tradition when he established his capital in Middle Egypt at Akhet-Aten, the modern Tell el-Amarna. This site has given its name to the Amarna Age as a convenient description of the fifteenth and fourteenth centuries B.C. when Amenhotep III and IV ruled over Egypt. At the beginning of the Amarna period proper, the Mitanni were still maintaining a balance of power between the Hittites and the Egyptians. Syria was garrisoned by Mitanni forces, who were peaceful allies of Egypt, but

Palestine was an Egyptian vassal with one or two spheres of Hittite influence. The Mitanni were rapidly disappearing as a world power, but despite this fact neither the Babylonians, the Hittites nor the Assyrians were as yet in a position to challenge the forces of the Egyptians.

During the middle of the Amarna Age the Hittite empire attained the peak of its influence. By the time of Suppiluliumas I (c. 1375-1335 B.C.) iron ore was being smelted in the province of Kizzuwatna in south-eastern Asia Minor on a scale which merits the designation of the beginning of the Iron Age. Like his predecessors, Suppiluliumas utilized this procedure for military as well as civil purposes, and with his weapons and iron-fitted chariots he extended his imperial rule over Upper Mesopotamia and across Syria as far south as the Lebanon range. But although Suppiluliumas may have recognized, as the Egyptians themselves did, that their power was already in decline at the beginning of the Amarna Age, he was still not prepared to risk a military confrontation of significant proportions with the Egyptian forces.

The peace which Egypt had imposed upon Canaan was combined with an administrative system designed to ensure the loyalty of the petty kings of Palestine, while at the same time affording them some measure of autonomy. Considerable light has been shed on the way in which the Egyptians administered their holdings in Canaan by the discovery at Tell el-Amarna of an important batch of early international diplomatic documents.[10] This correspondence was found in 1887 by an Egyptian peasant woman, and consisted of diplomatic communications from Mitanni, Babylonian and other rulers to Amenhotep III and IV. Of the 370 tablets which were recovered, about 150 originated in Palestine, most of which complained that the Habiru were overrunning the land and requested the immediate help of pharaoh in maintaining Egyptian control of southern Canaan.

These letters were invariably written with the courtesy which contemporary Near Eastern correspondence demanded. They dealt with matters which included social affairs, political considerations, enquiries concerning the health of the pharaoh, and the exchange of gifts and slaves. One document, written to Amenhotep III, dealt in a most tactful manner with the delicate subject of a certain Babylonian princess who had been given in marriage to the pharaoh, but who had not been seen or recognized subsequently by anyone from Babylon. This restrained enquiry about the fate of the princess was met with a jocular reply from Amenhotep III, who said that the ambassadors which the Babylonian king, Kadashman-Bal, had sent to Egypt never came near the royal court, and that in any event they were prejudiced. The final admonition to the enquirer was that he should send an ambassador "who knows your sister" so as to be reassured about her fate.

Another letter, from the land of Ube (probably the Hobah of Genesis 14: 15), was written by a certain Itadama, assuring the pharaoh of help against the incursions of the Habiru:

> "To the king my lord . . . Namyauza has delivered us to the Habiru all the king's cities in the land of Kadesh and Ube. Nevertheless, I will march forth and . . . will restore these places from the Habiru to the king, that I may show myself subject to Him."

The diminishing influence which the Egyptians were able to exert upon Syria and Palestine during this period gave the petty princes of those regions the opportunity for political intrigue and internecine strife in pursuit of personal ambition. From the Tell el-Amarna tablets it is clear that the rulers of the small city-states in Syria and Palestine spent a great deal of their time in denouncing each other to the Egyptian pharaoh, and endeavouring

PLATE 5. The Taylor Prism of Sennacherib. A cuneiform chronicle of events in the reign of the Assyrian monarch Sennacherib (*c.* 705-681 B.C.).

(By courtesy of the Trustees of the British Museum.)

PLATE 6. Meneptah of Egypt (*c.* 1230 B.C.). A celebrated pharaoh whose exploits in Canaan and the East were recorded on the Meneptah *stele*.

(*By courtesy of the Trustees of the British Museum.*)

PLATE 7. Babylonian Chronicle Tablet. This fragment contains the
account of the capture of Jerusalem by Nebuchadnezzar's forces on
16th March, 597 B.C.

(*By courtesy of the Trustees of the British Museum.*)

PLATE 8. A Boundary Stone from the time of Nebuchadnezzar I.
It depicts deities and a variety of other objects.
(*By courtesy of the Trustees of the British Museum.*)

to obtain aid from him to further their own plans for local conquests.

The rapidly weakening position in which Egypt found herself made it both undesirable and impossible for her to expend military forces upon enterprises which, in the end, could only do her further harm. In refusing to send more than the promise of aid to the clamouring Canaanite princes, the Egyptians were conscious of the threat to their own security posed by the evident decline in political and military influence of the Mitanni in northern Syria, and they looked with some concern at the possibility of Hittite expansion in the area.

Perhaps the most significant element in the rule of Amenhotep IV was his religious reformation. He broke with the worship of Amun and all the older deities, removed their names from monuments and proclaimed the sole worship of the god Aten. He even changed his own name from Amenhotep (Amenophis) to Ikhnaton, because the former comprised in part the divine name Amen (Amun). In one of the Tell el-Amarna tombs there was found the magnificent Hymn to the Sun,[11] which enshrined the spirituality of the new faith in beautiful words reminiscent of Psalm 104.

When Ikhnaton died at an early age, the suppressed Amun cult came to power again and swept aside his reforms in a frenzy of internal revolution. But by this time the Egyptian hold over Syria and Palestine was diminishing, and from the Tell el-Amarna tablets it appears that many of the small Canaanite city-states were at odds with each other. The Mitanni, the north Syrian ally of the Egyptians, were conquered and largely absorbed by Suppiluliumas, who thus became overlord of the north Syrian states. It is therefore quite probable that political motives alone prompted the beautiful Nefertiti to contract a marriage with a son of Suppiluliumas, and as such it would constitute an interesting commentary upon the internal weakness of Egypt, which hitherto had strictly forbidden its women to marry foreigners. A serious international crisis was precipitated when the prospective bridegroom was murdered on his way to Egypt by loyalist elements, and the situation was only saved by the accession of Tutankhaton to the throne of Egypt. This man was the son-in-law of Ikhnaton, who, in compliance with the wishes of the now-dominant Amun cult, changed his name to Tutankhamun. He reigned for only about eight years (c. 1352-1344 B.C.), but in gratitude for the restoration of the Amun priesthood he was given a splendid burial in the Valley of the Kings.

The opulence and magnificence of the Amarna Age was revealed to modern eyes when Howard Carter discovered and excavated the tomb in 1922. According to the excavators, an ante-room to the burial chamber proper seemed, from the profusion of strange animals, furniture, statues and objects of gold, to comprise an entire museum in itself. Perhaps the most remarkable piece of furniture was the throne of Tutankhamun, which was constructed of wood overlaid with gold. Its back panel depicted the king and queen wearing their splendid robes, which were reproduced on gold by means of inlaid faience, coloured glass and precious stones. Beyond the room was a shrine and the burial chamber proper, and these were opened on 18th February 1923 before a distinguished audience. The walls of the shrine were covered with gold leaf and inscribed with magical texts which were intended to protect the deceased king. The burial chamber lay to the east of the shrine and was separated by doors which opened readily on their hinges. A second shrine was encountered at this point and beyond it lay the sealed burial chamber, which, to the great relief of the excavators, had not been pillaged in antiquity. An annexe contained magnificent gold and ebony statues, boxes and chests inlaid with gold and semi-precious stones, and other elegant and costly objects.

The canopic shrine was opened the following season to reveal an immense, yellow quartzite sarcophagus intact, covered with religious texts and topped with a rose granite lid. When the latter was removed, a golden effigy of the king was revealed which filled the entire sarcophagus. Around the symbols on the forehead had been placed a small wreath of flowers, the last farewell gift of the sorrowing young widow Ankhesenamun to her departed husband. This coffin enclosed a second and a third, the last being of solid gold adorned with jewels, and of such superb design and execution as to constitute by far the most exquisite object of its kind in the world today. Inside lay the mummy of the king, his face covered with a mask of beaten gold and his body adorned with a great many beautiful objects, an eloquent testimony to the esteem in which Tutankhamun had been held. This fascinating and magnificent discovery has confirmed a great many things found in the Egyptian *Book of the Dead*, and in particular has shown the splendid nature of the burials accorded to those pharaohs who brought the people back to their "old time religion".

The Nineteenth Dynasty was founded by Haremhab (*c.* 1345-1308 B.C.), who held the Hittite forces at bay and instituted certain domestic reforms. Under Ramses I (*c.* 1303-1302 B.C.) and his son Seti I (*c.* 1302-1290 B.C.), a number of military campaigns were undertaken in Palestine against the Canaanites and Hittites, while Ramses II (*c.* 1290-1224 B.C.) also fought against the Hittites with considerable success. As a result, a non-aggression treaty between Hattusilis III and Ramses II was concluded in 1280 B.C., in which both parties recognized the Orontes as their common frontier. For the first time in Egyptian history a Hittite princess became queen

of Egypt by marrying Ramses II, son of Seti I, about
1267 B.C., and thus the Hittites gained a resounding
diplomatic triumph at the expense of a weakened Egypt.
In the end, however, this turn of events proved to have
little positive effect upon Hittite fortunes, for about
1200 B.C. the Hittite New Empire collapsed under a
series of attacks from the Sea Peoples,[12] and those
Hittites who survived fled to Syria and Palestine.

Early in the Nineteenth Dynasty, Ramses II moved his
capital from Thebes to the old Hyksos city of Tanis
(Avaris) and began to enlarge it. This constructional
activity seems to have taken place at a time when the
Hebrews were in captivity in Egypt,[13] and excavations
at Tell el-Retabah, the ancient city of Pithom,[14] showed
that the massive walls of that period were made of
"bricks without straw". The Egyptian store city, known
to the Hebrews as Raamses, was in fact Tanis,[15] the
capital of the Nineteenth Dynasty and, since the Old
Testament account used the name by which the city
was known for a period of two centuries only (c. 1300-
1100 B.C.), it is probable that the Hebrew tradition of
the enslavement, and subsequent exodus of the Israelites
under Moses, actually dated from this time.

If Ramses II was the pharaoh of the Hebrew oppress-
ion, his thirteenth son Meneptah would have been the
Egyptian ruler at the time of the Exodus. This pharaoh
was endeavouring to shore up his tottering Hittite ally,
who was succumbing rapidly to the onslaught of the Sea
Peoples, and at the same time was occupied closer to
home in repelling a threatened invasion of Libyans and
Sea Peoples along his western frontier. A victory paean
which commemorated this latter campaign ended with
what is the only mention of Israel in the entire corpus of
Egyptian literature.[16] This "Meneptah *stele*" would
therefore preclude a date much beyond 1220 B.C. for
the final entry of the Israelites into Canaan, and would

suggest a thirteenth rather than a fifteenth century B.C. date for the Hebrew exodus from Egypt.

The Nineteenth Dynasty terminated with a succession of feeble kings and about 1200 B.C. a Syrian adventurer gained the throne of Egypt. The Twentieth Dynasty (c. 1197-1090 B.C.) saw Ramses III as its most prominent pharaoh. Egypt was threatened at this time with invasion by the same forces as those which had brought about the collapse of the Hittite New Empire, but the situation was saved after three desperate battles[17] which forced the invaders to settle in the coastal region of south-west Palestine. Here they became known as Philistines and were, in fact, related to earlier immigrants in that area. For a time Ramses III regained a measure of control over Syria and the Palestinian lowlands, but this was relinquished when he was killed in a harîm-conspiracy about 1164 B.C.

The succeeding kings of the Dynasty, all of whom were named Ramses, were weak, and this unfortunate situation resulted in economic inflation, strikes and civil unrest. A series of tomb robberies which began about 1225 B.C. went on for a whole generation, the consequence of which was that all the royal tombs at Thebes were thoroughly looted. The priests of the Amun cult became increasingly independent of the king and the Dynasty ended with an enfeebled pharaoh a virtual palace prisoner, controlled by the viziers of Upper and Lower Egypt, the high priest of Amun and the army commander. With the death of this pharaoh, Ramses XI, the imperial power of ancient Egypt came to an end, and Egypt never again regained her dominance in the eastern Mediterranean world. Despite some military forays into Palestine and Syria, and political intrigue against the successive world powers of Assyria, Babylonia and Persia, the Egyptians were completely unable to attain to any further degree of real control in Asia.

CHAPTER 4

The Near East to 538 B.C.

The weakening of Egyptian influence in the Near East at the end of the Imperial period gave scope for the rise of a minor power which perpetuated some of the technological traditions of the Hittites. This group, the Philistines, were of non-Semitic stock, having migrated over a period of time from the Aegean, particularly from ancient Caphtor (Crete), to Canaan about 1175 B.C. Their chief occupational strength was restricted to the Gaza region, although they had been represented in small settlements in Canaan as far back as the period of the Hebrew patriarch Abraham, whose migration from Ur of the Chaldees to Palestine most probably occurred during the nineteenth century B.C.

The Philistines were first mentioned under the designation *prst* in the annals of Ramses III for his fifth and later years inscribed in his temple to Amon near Thebes. The annals mentioned his campaign against the invading group of Libyans and others known as the Sea Peoples, of whom the *prst* were one. Having settled in south-west Palestine, a name by which ancient Canaan became known after the twelfth century B.C. Philistine occupation, the invaders established a confederation of five cities in the Gaza region, upon which their military strength largely depended.

Archaeological excavations in Philistine territory have shown that it is clearly a mistake to regard the Philistines as synonymous with barbarity or cultural deficiency, as is so frequently done in common speech. A type of pottery recovered from late second millennium B.C. levels at Philistine sites has its own special characteristics, notably in terms of the decorations, which show marked affinities with Aegean styles. Locally made pottery from sites in Cyprus dated about 1225-1175 B.C., which also derives from Aegean sources, most probably represents the precursor of Philistine pottery. Clay coffins with faces moulded in relief, found at Beth-shan, can also be attributed to the Philistines, as can the shields, swords and triangular daggers depicted as Philistine armour on the relief in the mortuary temple of Ramses II at Thebes.

Quite aside from this, however, the Philistines exerted an important economic influence in the Near East through their arrival in Palestine at the transition from the Bronze Age to the Iron Age. They had learned the uses of iron from the Hittites, who had controlled the manufacture and export of that metal until their empire collapsed about 1200 B.C. At this point, the Philistines acquired a monopoly of the supply of iron and used it to fashion both agricultural implements and military weapons, a situation which gave them an undoubted technological advantage over the Egyptians and also over some of their less powerful neighbours such as the Israelites.[1]

The latter nation had arisen gradually over many centuries from the stock of the Hebrew patriarchs Abraham, Isaac and Jacob. It was most probably at the beginning of the Hyksos regime in Egypt that the Hebrews migrated to the Goshen region of the Nile Delta, since the local colour which is evident in the Old Testament accounts of the career of Joseph[2] is in full accord with this period of Asiatic domination of Egypt. Certainly, if the Egyptians had been in full control of their country at the time, their narrow nationalistic

attitudes would never have allowed a talented Semite
such as Joseph to rise to the office of Grand Vizier.[3]

All that is known about this period of Hebrew history
is found in the early books of the Old Testament, and
nothing has been preserved from Egyptian sources.
Quite possibly, some records of Hebrew achievements
were expunged when all traces of Hyksos rule were
obliterated at the beginning of the New Kingdom
period, but there is no firm evidence for this supposition.
However, the Book of Exodus makes it clear that a
reversal of Hebrew fortunes in Egypt occurred after the
death of Joseph,[4] and the expatriate Israelites found themselves in bondage, along with some Habiru and other
national elements, to the massive constructional schemes
of the New Kingdom period.

The circumstances of contemporary life lend firm
support to the Old Testament narratives of the Israelite
captivity in Egypt,[5] from which the unhappy Semites
were delivered under the leadership of Moses, the celebrated Hebrew lawgiver. After escaping into the Sinai
Peninsula, the Israelites entered into a spiritual relationship with God, patterned along the lines of second
millennium B.C. international treaties and known as a
covenant. A generation of wandering in the Sinai
Peninsula was followed by the conquest of certain
Transjordanian states and the entrance into Canaan,
their Promised Land, by way of Jericho.

Evidence for the rapid occupation of Palestine, as
depicted in the Book of Joshua, has been furnished by
archaeological discoveries at Ai, Bethel, Lachish, Debir
and Hazor, where clear indications of destruction at
thirteenth century B.C. levels were uncovered.[6] Once the
principal centres of habitation had been occupied, the
invading Israelites turned their attention to consolidating
their territorial gains and suppressing any attempts at
Canaanite resurgence. Overall national leadership by

one man ceased with the death of Joshua, and the Hebrews fell increasingly under the influence of Phoenician-Canaanite culture. Archaeological discoveries at Ras Shamra (Ugarit) on the north coast of Syria have furnished much valuable information about Phoenician life in the fourteenth century B.C. and have made it abundantly clear that the Canaanite religion in particular was one of the most depraved and immoral in the entire ancient world.

While the dangers presented to the traditional faith of the Hebrews are familiar to readers of the Old Testament, the true nature of Canaanite cultic worship has latterly become much clearer as a result of an examination of the poetic texts from Ras Shamra. Although the list of gods is unfortunately so fluid in terms of function and personality as to make it extremely difficult on occasions to determine their exact inter-relationships, it is clearly evident that the cult was, in fact, a debased form of ritual polytheism.

One of its most prominent features was the lewd and depraved orgiastic character of its cultic procedures, and so attractive did Canaanite religion become to those who visited the land from other parts of the ancient Near East that elements of it ultimately infiltrated the highly conservative religious cults of Babylonia and Egypt, becoming associated to varying extents with the functions of local gods.

The supreme Canaanite deity was El, the "father of man", who was represented on a *stele* unearthed at Ras Shamra as standing with arms outstretched in blessing over the ruler of Ugarit. His consort Asherat, the Asherah of the Old Testament writers, was venerated as the mother of the fertility deity Baal, the overlord of rain and storm. The fertility goddess Anat was sometimes represented as a vicious, vindictive deity, who would slay young and old alike in a fiendish orgy of destruction.

This latter characterization was similar to those Egyptian sources which depicted Anat and Astarte as deities of violence and war, representing them naked astride galloping horses and waving weapons of destruction.

The twelfth century B.C. saw increasing Canaanite resistance to the conquering Israelites in many parts of Palestine, augmented by occasional forays against the Hebrews by nomadic tribes from the Transjordan region. To some extent the unrest in Canaan was the result of military weakness in post-Imperial Egypt, which itself continued to break up into smaller independent states. The low esteem into which Egypt had now fallen in the eyes of foreign nations can be illustrated by the story of Wen-Amun, who was sent to Phoenicia about 1100 B.C. by the high priest of Thebes to obtain cedar for the sacred boat of the god, and only accomplished his objective after a number of irritating delays and humiliating experiences.[7]

Although the Hebrews who occupied Canaan under Joshua were able to draw upon a tradition of over two centuries of sedentary occupation in the land of Goshen prior to the New Kingdom period of Egyptian history, they were by no means as advanced culturally as the native occupants of the land which they had conquered. Indeed, even the grandeur of the Canaanite walled towns filled the semi-nomadic Israelite invaders with awe. As one of their number was forced to admit "the cities are great and fenced up to heaven" (Deuteronomy 1 : 28).

Excavations indicate that the Israelites took over not merely the cities which the Canaanites had erected previously, but also the architectural styles of many of the buildings themselves. The reason for this turn of events was primarily because the Israelites, on their arrival in the Promised Land, were completely ignorant of the techniques involved in the construction of buildings, as their indifferent repairs and improvised patchings show clearly.

Large residences formerly owned by wealthy Canaanite families were divided up into apartments, which accommodated more than one family on most occasions and not infrequently also included some domesticated animals. Smaller houses were often built close by, generally without the slightest hint of any conformity to some type of rough town-planning and making for an extremely congested situation. Streets as such were seldom laid out in Israelite cities, and were actually nothing more than narrow alleys about 7 feet wide which wound in between houses and around corners without any specific plan. Pedestrians picked their way along these thoroughfares in single file, avoiding the ever-present filth underfoot and the equally undesirable encounters with asses, cattle and camels.

Bigger cities had special areas set aside for the use of shopkeepers, but they were in effect nothing more than untidy bazaars of a kind still encountered in some eastern cities. Here merchants would come with their caravans and, once the crowds of buyers and interested spectators had assembled, their wares would soon become the object of typical oriental haggling. Occasionally, foreign traders had a separate part of the city reserved for their business transactions, a situation reflected in the exchange which was negotiated between Damascus and Samaria during the reigns of Ahab of Israel and Benhadad of Damascus. Most merchants, however, clustered around the city gate in order to sell their goods and, since the gate was usually the only place in the city which was big enough to allow people to assemble, it was always highly congested and almost inevitably littered with refuse each day.

The mud and filth of the city streets was taken very much for granted by writers in the Old Testament (as with Isaiah 5: 25; 10: 6) and the accumulation of potsherds, damaged or crumbled bricks, household garbage, and the layer of dust and ashes which formed the normal surface of the lanes must have made walking a very risky and unpleasant affair each time it rained. In the heat of the summer the stench of putrefying material such as dead asses, which, according to Jeremiah 22: 19, were simply dragged along the street and thrown outside the gate of the city, was doubtless as unpleasant as it was unhygienic. Thus, it is small wonder that epidemics of various kinds broke out with devastating severity under such conditions, helped by the activities of flies, which first fed on putrefying material and then injected the contents of their probosces into food supplies, or on to the eyes of sleeping children to produce the widespread affliction of ophthalmia.

In peacetime the city population inevitably overflowed, since the cities themselves were tiny by comparison with their counterparts in Babylonia and Egypt. Thus Jerusalem was only 13 acres in area, Megiddo about the same, and Debir a mere $7\frac{1}{2}$ acres in extent. Outside these and other cities there grew up a collection of huts and tents, which were dotted about the grazing land stretching beyond the city walls. Sometimes a second fortified wall was constructed, as at Lachish, in an attempt to cope with some of the problems of overcrowding (though with limited success).

During the summer months when the heat of the city became intolerable, the majority of the populace moved outside the fortress to join the few permanent villagers in working in the fields and grazing their cattle. The congestion and filth of the cities was such that, from the ninth century B.C. onwards, the inhabitants spent as much time as possible in the surrounding countryside, only returning to their homes when the chill of winter weather made it desirable to do so.

Very often, the location of Israelite cities depended as much upon the presence of a reasonably stable water supply as on military or strategic considerations. In the early settlement period, the Israelites made extensive use of cisterns in order to augment natural springs in the area. By the time of the monarchy, they had learned the technique of lining their cisterns with waterproof lime plaster. This enabled them to collect and store rain water, and thus to build their cities at a greater distance from springs and streams, as at Lachish, where many houses had their own cisterns dug out of the solid rock.

In view of the general congestion, the noise which must have occurred in Israelite cities of the period under discussion can only be imagined. The "salutations in the market places" (Mark 12: 38) were only one small part of the ceremonial greetings beloved of oriental peoples for millennia. Apart from these expressions of courtesy and friendship, there were the strident cries of hawkers, pushing their way through narrow alleys and drowning out the chatter of friends, the shout of the water-merchant (cf. Isaiah 55: 1), the noises of the animals, the cries of children at play, and the incessant barking of dogs scavenging in the litter and garbage. Thus, while Israelite cities represented a degree of security for their inhabitants, they were by no means particularly healthy or desirable places in which to live.

Events in Palestine were dominated by the continuous clashes between the Israelites and various elements of the native population. In the eleventh century B.C. the Philistines presented an increasing threat to the Israelite economy, which was inferior technologically, and the general disunity of Hebrew society at this time prompted the people to demand a king. The prophet Samuel anointed Saul as the first ruler of Israel, but he became mentally ill and was unable to furnish proper leadership

against the marauding Philistines. David, the celebrated
Hebrew champion, ultimately succeeded Saul about
1011 B.C., and established his capital in Jerusalem,
which had been a Jebusite stronghold for at least a
millennium. David was a valiant warrior and conse-
quently an extremely popular figure. He enshrined all
the qualities of the ideal Hebrew aristocrat, but unfortunately was deficient in the ordering of his own household and suffered from fratricidal strife as a result. He
died about 970 B.C., a pathetic figure of senility. He was
succeeded by his son Solomon.

As a youth, this renowned Israelite king was profoundly religious by disposition and of great intellectual
ability, becoming legendary at a comparatively early age.
This situation was aided and abetted by the fact that there
was no other outstanding king in any of the Near
Eastern countries at that particular period, so that
Solomon gained no small portion of his reputation
through sheer default on the part of others.

Probably with political considerations in view,
Solomon married an Egyptian princess who came to live
at his court in Jerusalem, another indication of the
weakness of Egypt at this time which, under normal
conditions, would never have permitted Egyptian women
to leave their homeland and marry foreigners. Solomon
established twelve administrative districts in Palestine,
based upon Egyptian patterns, in order to diminish the
authority of the Hebrew tribes, and began a series of
military campaigns with the intention of securing the
borders of his kingdom. One such expedition was
launched against Hamath on the River Orontes in Syria,
some 120 miles north of Damascus, an area which had
formerly been under Hittite control.

The Aramean Dynasty of Hadad the Edomite was
proving a potential source of trouble for Solomon, particularly when Rezon, the commander of Hadad's

forces, seized control of Damascus. To counter this move Solomon fortified the ancient Bronze Age city of Hazor, constructed other strong points in the Lebanon region and established firm control over the caravan-route from Ezion-geber northward through the Arabah so as to thwart Edomite aspirations in this area. Whereas the more conservatively minded David had refused to utilize chariots as weapons of war, Solomon concentrated on building up a large force of chariotry, elements of which were stationed in towns such as Jerusalem, Gezer, Megiddo and Hazor.[8]

Solomon took advantage of the decline in Egyptian and Assyrian power to expand the economy of his vast realm. He continued the political alliance established between David and Hiram of Tyre, and obtained a monopoly of the entire caravan trade between Arabia and Syria. He built a large navy based on Ezion-geber and manned by Phoenician sailors, exploited the rich mineral resources of the Wadi Arabah and indulged in considerable smelting activity near Ezion-geber at the celebrated "King Solomon's mines".[9]

The first copper refinery ever to be excavated in the Near East was the one which had been constructed for King Solomon in the tenth century B.C. by Phoenician artisans. These drew upon a lengthy tradition of skill in the building of copper smelting furnaces and the refining of ore. The site of Ezion-geber (Tell el Kheleifeh), located between the hill-country of Sinai and the uplands of Edom, was by far the most suitable place for building a refinery, since it received the full benefit of the fierce windstorms which swept down the Wadi Arabah from the north.

Excavations at the site uncovered a building whose northern wall was completely blank except for two horizontal rows of holes. A series of air ducts ran through the middle of the main walls of the building and were linked to the upper row of holes to form flues. The ore was placed in crucibles inside the smelter and a brush or wood fire, which was made intensely hot by the draught, reduced the ore to ingots of a size convenient for shipment elsewhere.

The grandiose nature of the building projects which Solomon began in his kingdom has been revealed by excavations at Gezer and Megiddo. The latter site seems to have been one of his administrative centres, and in the tenth century B.C. was occupied by a fortified palace. The district officer had a residence in one of the towers which formed part of the defensive fortification, and there appears to have been generous provision made for the accommodation of horses and chariots. The masonry elements of the walls, though typical of the Solomonic era, reflected earlier Phoenician constructional techniques which have also been observed at such sites as Gezer, Lachish and Ezion-geber.

However, the most spectacular public works of the Solomonic period were to be found in his capital city of Jerusalem. Solomon reconstructed the Millo, a defensive outpost originally built by David at the northern end of the old city, and then proceeded to erect a complex of buildings which included the royal palace and the Temple. The latter was characteristically Phoenician in design, being, in fact, remarkably similar in ground plan to the remains of an eighth century B.C. chapel which was excavated at Tell Tainat in Syria.

However, the ambitious domestic programme of Solomon brought with it a serious degree of economic inflation, and when Rehoboam, the son and successor of Solomon, announced his intentions of increasing the burdens already imposed upon the Israelites by his father the nation split into two uneven portions. Ten and a half tribes in the north of Palestine formed the kingdom of Israel, and the remaining one and half tribes to the south became known as the kingdom of Judah. Taking advantage of this political crisis, Sheshonk I of Egypt (*c.* 940-914 B.C.), the powerful founder of the Twenty-second Dynasty, invaded Judah, destroyed several fortresses and carried away most of the Temple treasures from Jerusalem. This calamity dealt a serious economic blow to Judah from which it never really recovered.

In the meantime, the Aramean Dynasty of Damascus was gaining in strength and was becoming dominant in Syria. The discovery in 1940 of the inscribed *stele* of Benhadad in northern Syria has given general confirmation to the list of Syrian rulers mentioned in the Old Testament,[10] although the position of Rezon, founder of the Damascene State, is still uncertain. Rezon had escaped from a battle with King David[11] and had subsequently made Damascus the capital of the newly formed Aramean city-state of Aram. The political influence of the city grew rapidly, and by the time Benhadad I (*c.* 900-860 B.C.) came to power the Syrian regime was strong enough to receive a request from Asa of Judah for help against Baasha of Israel.

Benhadad responded vigorously to this appeal for help by driving Baasha back to his capital city of Tirzah, at the same time managing to gain control of the prosperous caravan routes to the ports of Phoenicia. This astute move enabled him to augment the economic prosperity of his own kingdom, and in so doing he was following the precedent established by Solomon in an earlier stage of the history of Judah.

The initial growth of Syrian power was aided by the ill-concealed hostility which existed between Israel and Judah, and also by the political instability of the Hebrew northern kingdom after the time of Jeroboam I (931-910 B.C.). Consequently, Benhadad I was able to demand the provision of merchants' quarters in Damascus as one

D

element of a treaty made with Ahab of Israel (874-853 B.C.).[12] The purpose of this agreement was to obtain the support of Israel for a coalition of city-states to oppose the rising power of Assyria under Ashurnasirpal II (883-859 B.C.) and Shalmaneser III (859-824 B.C.).

The northern kingdom of Israel had derived great benefit from the leadership of Omri (885-873 B.C.), the father of Ahab, who established a new dynasty, the *Bit-Humri* (House of Omri) of Assyrian cuneiform records. The capital city of Israel was moved to Samaria, which was fortified strongly, and an Israelite trading alliance was concluded with Phoenicia, partly in an attempt to offset the control which Syria had acquired over commercial dealings. Diplomatic links with Tyre were strengthened under Ahab and a non-aggression treaty was concluded with Judah so as to protect the southern borders of Israel.

The vigour which Omri displayed in his dealings with neighbouring kingdoms was revealed by the discovery of the Moabite Stone in 1868. This monument, a black basalt victory-*stele* erected by King Mesha of Moab at Dibon about 840 B.C., shows that Omri of Israel had managed to gain military control over northern Moab and was exacting heavy tribute during his reign:

"I am Mesha, son of Chemosh . . . king of Moab, the Dibonite . . . Omri, king of Israel . . . oppressed Moab for many days because Chemosh was angry with his land. And his son succeeded him, and he also said, 'I will oppress Moab' . . ."

At this time some form of contact was established with the Assyrians, for Israel was subsequently referred to in cuneiform records as *Bit-Humri* or "House of Omri", a designation which was also applied to Samaria, the capital city of the Israelites. About 855 B.C., Benhadad and his coalition of Syrian states launched an attack upon Samaria, but were repulsed with heavy losses. The following year a further Syrian attack at Aphek, east of the Sea of Galilee, resulted in a surprising defeat for Benhadad and, had the northern kingdom of Israel been able to seize the initiative, the Damascene Dynasty might not have survived for more than a few months. Unfortunately, the Israelites were deprived of this opportunity to liquidate their enemy by the sudden appearance of a powerful Assyrian expedition under Shalmaneser III against Palestine about 853 B.C.

While it was by no means unusual for numbers to be exaggerated when the course of a battle was being recorded by Near Eastern annalists, there seems to be no good reason for doubting that the coalition of Syrian kings at Qarqar could indeed rely on 2,000 chariots and 10,000 men as the contribution made by Ahab of Israel to the struggle against the common enemy. Though success was short lived, the victory at least halted the south-eastern advance of the Assyrian forces for several years. In the end, however, the military intervention of the coalition proved to be one of the principal reasons why the Assyrians determined to move in strength against the kingdom of Israel.

The Assyrians had become notorious in the Near East for the brutality with which they conducted their military campaigns, and the emergency situation which was thus precipitated upon Palestine compelled erstwhile enemies to ally against the invader. Ahab joined with Benhadad in a full-scale battle against the Assyrians at Qarqar on the River Orontes in 853 B.C., in which large numbers of Israelite chariots and Syrian foot-soldiers defeated the Assyrians. As was the normal Near Eastern custom, however, the latter claimed the victory for themselves in complete indifference to what the Palestinian coalition might have to say about the matter, and the description of the occasion from the Assyrian point of view has been preserved in the Monolith Inscription of Shalmaneser III.[13]

Following this defeat, the Assyrians withdrew to re-group and re-equip their forces, and in the interval the old hostility between Israel and Syria flared up once more. As a result, Ahab of Israel was killed in 853 B.C. while trying to recover Ramoth-gilead from Syrian control. The Hebrew prophet Elijah was commissioned to anoint a Damascene nobleman named Hazael as the future king of Syria, and when Benhadad died this king had to face a renewed Assyrian attack under Shalmaneser III in 843 B.C. Hazael lost large numbers of his troops while holding a pass in the Lebanon range, and was ultimately forced to withdraw to Damascus, where he was besieged for four years. Jehu of Israel (841-813 B.C.) withdrew from the Syrian coalition before the main attack on Hazael took place, preferring to pay heavy tribute to the Assyrians rather than risk decimation by their armies. The siege of Damascus was lifted when the enemy had to withdraw from Syria to defend the nor-thern border of Assyria, after which Hazael subjugated most of Israel and gained control of the Philistine Plain.

The kingdom of Israel reached the height of its pros-perity under Joash (798-781 B.C.) and Jeroboam II (781-743 B.C.). Benhadad III of Syria was compelled to defend himself against an attack by Zakir, king of Hamath, who was endeavouring to usurp the throne, and this fact, combined with the weakness of com-temporary Assyria and Egypt, removed any military threat to the kingdoms of Israel and Judah. Conse-quently, these latter nations experienced an almost unprecedented economic upsurge, and a rich mercantile class which was acquiring large profits from Phoenician commercial enterprises appeared in Hebrew society.

However, hand in hand with prosperity came an alarming degree of corruption in the land, a situation about which Amos, Micah and other eighth century B.C. Hebrew prophets protested vigorously. Archaeological excavations at various sites in Palestine have confirmed the splendour and luxury of this general period, and have also given good ground for the strictures of the Hebrew prophets. At Samaria, for example, an expedition in 1910 recovered some sixty-three potsherds which, when deciphered, consisted of administrative documents recording shipments of wine and oil to Samaria. The mention in the potsherds of "pure clarified wine" and "refined oil" typify the exaggerated demands of the luxury-loving elite of the northern capital, and demonstrate the extent to which they had moved away from the peasant ideals of Hebrew society.

The prophet Amos saw that the nation had been corrupted by the sensuality and immorality of pagan Canaanite worship, and had replaced the advanced morality of the Mosaic legislation with a gross, blatant materialism. As a result, the rich landowners and the newly arrived mercantile class were competing for the dubious honour of crushing the lowly tenant-farmers and peasants out of existence. So corrupt had society become that it was possible for the wealthy to bribe the judges to render decisions in their favour if their own attempts at depriving people of their lands were challenged in the courts.

This cry for social justice, enunciated so loudly by Amos, was emphasized equally by the prophet Micah, who took the side of the small landowners near Jerusalem. Isaiah noted how the wealthy landowners had taken every advantage of their poorer brethren and, so far from expressing the intense social concern manifested in the Mosaic Law, had oppressed them without mercy. His denunciations were directed especially at Jerusalem, the capital city of Judah, and his prophetic oracles condemned the corruption rampant among the religious leaders of his day and the gross miscarriages of justice condoned by those allegedly dedicated to upholding the law. For Micah, the crowning insult was that all this was carried on in an atmosphere of false religiosity, and it was small wonder that he could look forward to national catastrophe unless men learned to do justice, love mercy and walk humbly with their God (Micah 6: 8).

After the death of Adadnirari III in 782 B.C., Assyria was ruled by three weak monarchs, Shalmaneser IV (782-773 B.C.), Ashurdan III (772-755 B.C.) and Ashurnirari V (754-745 B.C.). Shortly after Jeroboam II died, a powerful warrior named Tiglathpileser III (745-727 B.C.) usurped the Assyrian throne and took immediate steps to contain the kingdom of Urartu, which was influencing the Syrian city-states against Assyrian rule. During the reign of Menahem of Israel (752-741 B.C.), Tiglathpileser III appeared on the frontier of the northern kingdom and made Menahem his tributary, together with the rulers of Tyre, Carchemish, Hamath, Byblos and Damascus.

Tiglathpileser III mounted a further campaign against Palestine in response to an appeal by Ahaz of Judah (731-715 B.C.) for help against a threatened attack by an alliance of Syrian and Israelite forces. Before the Assyrian armies could arrive, however, the coalition placed Jerusalem under siege, and this was only lifted when Tiglathpileser III marched on Dasmascus late in 733 B.C. When this city fell the following year, the Assyrian ruler conducted a campaign against other fortified cities in Palestine, with the result that Galilee was captured, the Philistine Plain was occupied, and sites such as Kadesh, Hazor and Ijon were destroyed. At the same time, Assyrian territorial holdings were extended to include the Sabeans and Arabia.

Using captive labour, Tiglathpileser III erected a

magnificent palace at Galah, from which reliefs depicting the king and his campaigns have been recovered. With the death of Rezin and the overthrow of Damascus, the Aramean Dynasty came to an end, leaving the nations in the Near East at the mercy of the Assyrian armies. Damascus itself became a minor city in the Assyrian province of Hamath and, although it continued to exert an economic influence in subsequent times, it never again recovered its political stature.

Tiglathpileser III was succeeded by his son, Shal-maneser V (727-722 B.C.), who besieged Samaria when Hoshea of Israel (731-722 B.C.) refused to pay tribute to Assyria and sought instead to ally with Egypt. The identity of the particular pharaoh, described in the Hebrew records as "So, king of Egypt",[14] is uncertain. He is not the Sib'e, commander of the Egyptian forces mentioned in the annals of Sargon of Assyria, nor is the person concerned the pharaoh Shabaka (c. 716-702 B.C.), a ruler from the later Ethiopian period. Quite possibly, he was Osorkon IV (c. 727-716 B.C.), the last pharaoh of the Twenty-second Dynasty at Zoan (Tanis-Avaris).

Before Samaria collapsed in 722 B.C. under Assyrian attack, Shalmaneser V was succeeded by Sargon II (722-705 B.C.), who overthrew the ruling king of Israel, Hoshea, and took the northern tribes into captivity, an event which terminated the existence of Israel as a separate kingdom. Hard on the heels of this occurrence came unrest in Assyria, which was settled in 721 B.C. by the granting of certain privileges to the citizens of Asshur. In 720 B.C., Sargon II marched against the Chaldean ruler Marduk-apla-iddina II, the Merodach-Baladan of the Old Testament historical records, who had seized the Babylonian throne. An inconclusive battle at Der halted the advance of some Elamite and Arab tribes which had rushed to support Marduk-apla-iddina, but in the end the latter still occupied the throne of Babylon and ruled from 721 to 710 B.C.

An anti-Assyrian coalition, comprising the western provincial states of Arpad, Damascus, Simirra and Samaria, was defeated at Qarqar in northern Syria in 720 B.C. This eventuality presented a serious threat to the kingdom of Judah, which under Hezekiah (716-686 B.C.) had allied with Babylon against Assyria and had also made certain political overtures to Egypt. Sargon swept down to the Egyptian border and routed an army sent to help the alliance of the city-states. He subsequently deported a large part of the population of Samaria and rebuilt the city as the capital of a new Assyrian province of Samaria.

In 716 B.C. Sargon conducted a campaign against the Arabs in the Sinai region, and four years later crushed another Syro-Palestinian revolt against Assyria. On other fronts, Sargon defeated the Mannaeans and Rusas of Urartu between 719 and 714 B.C., and raided the positions of the hill-tribes of Media in 710 and 707 B.C. One of his last campaigns was conducted against Marduk-apla-iddina II, who was forced to flee for safety to Elam. Sargon II was assassinated in 705 B.C. and succeeded by his son Sennacherib (705-681 B.C.), who defeated the resurgent Marduk-apla-iddina II and his allies in battles at Cutha and Kish, and occupied the throne of Babylon. After some raids against the hill-peoples of the east, he marched westward, where an anti-Assyrian coalition backed by Egypt was gaining in strength. The leader, Hezekiah of Judah, had managed to obtain control of the pro-Assyrian city of Ekron, had fortified Jerusalem against the possibility of Assyrian attack and had also called upon the Egyptians for military assistance.

The third campaign of Sennacherib, conducted in the fourteenth year of Hezekiah (401 B.C.), was directed against this alliance. The Assyrians swept to the Mediterranean coast in 701 B.C. and reduced Sidon, Joppa, Timnath, Byblos and other centres of opposition. An Egyptian force sent to relieve these cities was itself compelled to withdraw and Jerusalem was placed under siege. In order to gain time to organize resistance, Hezekiah paid tribute to the Assyrians and released Padi, king of Ekron, whom he had been holding prisoner. The annals of Sennacherib make no mention of the conclusion of the siege or the withdrawal of the Assyrian army, but the Old Testament records[15] seem to point to some sort of epidemic or plague as the reason for the removal of the Assyrian forces.

In their characteristic fashion, the annals of Sennacherib described the way in which the inhabitants of Jerusalem had succumbed to Assyrian might:

"As regards Hezekiah the Jew, who did not submit to my yoke, forty-six of his strong fortified cities, as well as the smaller cities of the neighbourhood . . . I besieged and captured . . . Himself, like a caged bird, I shut up in Jerusalem, his royal city . . . As regards Hezekiah, the frightening splendour of my majesty overwhelmed him . . . and his mercenary troops . . . deserted him."

In 700 B.C. the Assyrians marched again to Babylon to quell a revolt. Sennacherib placed his own son Ashshur-nadin-shum on the throne, who ruled for a few years until he was captured by the Elamites. From 694 B.C. Sennacherib mounted several attacks against this marauding people and ultimately sacked Babylon in 689 B.C. On other frontiers he endeavoured to secure Assyrian supremacy by invading Cilicia, and raiding Arab positions to the south and east of Damascus.

Sennacherib was assassinated by his sons in 681 B.C. and was succeeded by Esarhaddon (681-669 B.C.), the crown prince. This man continued the policy of Senna-

cherib in the western provinces, exacting heavy tribute
from the kings of Syria, Palestine and the Transjordanian countries. Tirhakah of Egypt had been inciting
certain of the cities in the Philistine Plain to revolt
against Assyria, but Esarhaddon proved more than equal
to the occasion when he inflicted a resounding defeat
upon the Egyptian armies about 671 B.C., after which
Egypt became an Assyrian dependency. Esarhaddon
died in 669 B.C. at Harran while on his way home to
quell intrigue in his capital. He was succeeded by his
son Ashurbanipal (669-630 B.C.).

Under this competent and cultivated leader, the power
of Assyria reached its height. Although Ashurbanipal
was a renowned warrior, he was also a man of letters
and made important cultural contributions to the
Assyrian empire. He established an enormous library at
Nineveh in which he housed as much of the historical,
scientific, legal and religious literature of Babylonia and
Assyria as his emissaries could collect. This library was
unearthed in 1853. Ashurbanipal consolidated the gains
which his father had made in Syria and Egypt and,
having conquered Memphis and Thebes in 663 B.C.,
made an Egyptian prince named Necho the vassal
pharaoh.

Internal strife shook Assyria about 652 B.C., with
Babylon taking the lead in causing political disturbances.
Using the situation to their own advantage, the Egyptians, Phoenicians and some of the Transjordanian kingdoms also revolted against Assyria, but this movement
subsided when Babylon was crushed in 648 B.C. When
Ashurbanipal died in 630 B.C., the power of Assyria
dwindled rapidly and the empire was soon invaded from
the north by the Scythians, a barbarous nomadic group,
who pushed west and south through Palestine in the
direction of Egypt.

In 616 B.C. the Babylonians, led by Nabopolassar

(626-605 B.C.), allied with Medan forces in an attack upon Assyria. Asshur, the capital city, fell in 614 B.C. and after two years of bitter fighting Nineveh was also captured. The remnants of the Assyrian army retreated westward to Harran, which fell in 610 B.C., and with its collapse came the end of the Assyrian empire. In 609 B.C. the Egyptian pharaoh Necho went to Harran to the aid of the beleaguered Assyrians, killing Josiah of Judah *en route* at Megiddo when he tried to intercept the Egyptian forces. Necho arrived too late to prevent the fall of Harran and was subsequently defeated by Nebuchadnezzar II (605-562 B.C.) at Carchemish.

The Babylonian armies then advanced towards the Egyptian border and made Jehoiakim of Judah (605-597 B.C.) their tributary. After three years Jehoiakim rebelled against Babylon, despite the warnings of the prophet Jeremiah,[16] and in 597 B.C. the Babylonian forces swept down upon Jerusalem. The Temple was pillaged and Jehoiachin, who had succeeded his father as king a few months earlier, was blinded and carried captive to Babylon by Nebuchadnezzar. The discovery in 1956 by D. J. Wiseman of four additional tablets of the Babylonian Chronicle furnished the first extra-Biblical account of the fall of Jerusalem, and in addition provided certain details of events occurring between 626 and 594 B.C.[17] Further Babylonian raids on Palestine occurred in 587 and 581 B.C., after which the southern kingdom of Judah was left largely depopulated and desolate.

Unexpected light was thrown upon the last days of the kingdom of Judah by the discovery at Lachish (Tell ed-Duweir) in 1935 of eighteen potsherds inscribed in the ancient Canaanite script. In 1938 three more ostraca were uncovered at the same site, a small guard-room which had been built just outside the city gate. The potsherds consisted of letters and lists of names from the period immediately preceding the destruction of Jerusalem in 587 B.C. by Babylonian and Chaldean forces. Most of the ostraca can actually be dated from the autumn of 589 B.C., since they belonged chronologically to the layer of ash which resulted from the final destruction of Lachish by Nebuchadnezzar.

The majority of the documents were found to be in a bad state of preservation, but when deciphered proved to consist of dispatches written from a military outpost north of Lachish by an individual named Hoshaiah to a certain Joash, who was probably a staff officer in charge of the defences at Lachish. One potsherd complained about the way in which certain communications sent out by the court officials were having a demoralizing effect upon the populace generally, and pointed to the low state of morale in Jerusalem immediately before its destruction by the Babylonians.

Once Nebuchadnezzar had reduced opposition to Babylon in the western provinces, he set about making the Babylonian-Chaldean regime the most splendid in the ancient world. Using captive peoples from various countries, he embarked upon the restoration and enlargement of Babylon, his capital city. Nine-tenths of the total area consisted of parklands and gardens, while the remainder was occupied by temples, public buildings and private dwellings. When construction had been completed, the city was surrounded by a heavily fortified double wall, reinforced by means of an additional brickwork barrier, and access was controlled by eight massive gates. The celebrated "hanging gardens", which were actually raised terraces, and an enormous *ziggurat* were among the many magnificent buildings constructed during the Babylonian New Empire period (*c.* 612-539 B.C.).

The splendour and industry of the age of Nebuchadnezzar made him a legend in his own time, and contemporary records, written in the first person, testified to the great achievements of the day:

> "The produce of the lands, the products of the mountains, the bountiful wealth of the sea, within her (i.e., *his kingdom*) I gathered . . . great quantities of grain beyond measure I stored up in her. At that time the palace, my royal abode . . . I rebuilt in Babylon . . . great cedars I brought from Lebanon the beautiful forest, to roof it . . ."

When Nebuchadnezzar died in 562 B.C. he was succeeded by his son Amel-Marduk, whose accession was marked by a waning of Babylonian power. At this time any threat to the stability of the empire was purely internal since, although the Egyptian Saitic period (663-525 B.C.) saw some attempt to revive the ancient military glory of Egypt after 600 B.C. by means of Greek mercenary troops, its impact was short lived. Under Ahmose II (570-526 B.C.) a non-aggression treaty appears to have been made with the Babylonians, for thereafter until the fall of Babylon they were allied against the increasing threat of Median military interference in Babylonia.

In 560 B.C. Amel-Marduk was murdered by his brother-in-law Neriglisar, who reigned for four years. His son occupied the throne for a few months in 556 B.C. before being murdered. One of the conspirators, Nabonidus, succeeded him and reigned until 539 B.C. He was a cultured man who, like Ashurbanipal of Assyria, collected ancient inscriptions and other similar artefacts. About 523 B.C., before setting out for a series of campaigns in Arabia, he made his son Belshazzar co-regent. Thereafter, Nabonidus lived at the oasis of Teima in Arabia for a number of years, having quarrelled with the priestly hierarchy in Babylon.

From about 540 B.C. intrigue at the royal court seriously weakened the power of Belshazzar. This made possible the dramatic rise to power of Cyrus, king of Anshan, a vassal state under Astyages of Media. Cyrus revolted against his overlord in 549 B.C. and three years later repeated his initial success against the forces of Croesus, king of Lydia, thereby gaining control of Asia Minor as well as Media. In 539 B.C. he attacked Babylon, and is reported to have diverted the course of the River Euphrates at Opis preparatory to his assault so that his soldiers could enter the city along the river-bed. The Chaldean armies were routed, Belshazzar was killed when Babylon was captured and Cyrus the Persian became the undisputed master of the largest empire known to the ancient world.

At the time of writing, archaeological findings have not been entirely successful in establishing an identification which would resolve the problems attaching to the mention of "Darius the Mede" in Daniel 5: 30. From the latter source it would appear that he received the government on the death of Belshazzar, the last king of Babylon, being made ruler of the Chaldeans at the age of sixty-two. He bore the title of "king" and the years were marked in terms of his reign, according to the normal scribal procedure. He appointed an administrative corps of 120 subordinate governors under three presiding officers, one of whom was Daniel himself. Since Darius was a contemporary of Cyrus the Persian, he obviously cannot be identified with Darius I, king of Persia and Babylon from 522 to 486 B.C.

However, there can be little doubt that "Darius the Mede" was in fact an historical personage, and the discovery of one of the Nabonidus texts at Harran which referred to the "king of the Medes" raises the question as to whether this designation may possibly have constituted an alternative name for Cyrus. What appears to be a much more satisfactory explanation has been provided by the Nabonidus Chronicle itself, a cuneiform record of contemporary events, which mentioned two individuals, Ugbaru and Gubaru, both of whom were involved in the fighting which led to the fall of Babylon. A careful reading of the Chronicle suggests that Ugbaru was the governor of Gutium who conquered Babylon in 539 B.C. and died shortly afterwards.

It would thus appear that the other person mentioned, Gubaru, was appointed to the position of governor of Babylon by Cyrus the Persian, and that he ruled the city for about fourteen years, being designated in the Book of Daniel by the title of "Darius the Mede". It is not too much to hope that future archaeological discoveries will resolve this intriguing historical problem, since the title in its Old Testament form does not occur anywhere outside the Book of Daniel.

CHAPTER 5

Persia and Greece

The revolt instigated by Cyrus II against the king of
Media resulted in the establishment of the Achaemenian
empire. The Achaemenians traced their origins, which
are admittedly rather obscure, to Achaemenes, the father
of Teispes and grandfather of Cyrus I. At some period
after 652 B.C., this latter ruler opposed Ashurbanipal of
Assyria, but was forced to come to terms when the
Assyrian ruler brought his forces to Babylon in an attempt
to crush the influence of his twin brother Shamash-
shum-ukin, who occupied the throne of Babylon.
Having established his hold upon Anatolia, Cyrus II
turned his attention to India and by 542 B.C. had gained
firm control over the north-western part of that vast
land. Once Babylonia had been conquered, the territory
was divided up into large regions governed by satraps,
an old Persian term for "viceroys".

The Persian subjugation of Anatolia in 546 B.C. furnished the first significant contact which the conquerors
had with the Greek peoples. This race had arisen towards
the end of the third millennium B.C. as the result of
settlement by migrant groups in various parts of the
southern end of the Balkan peninsula, western Asia
Minor and the islands of the Aegean Sea. In the prehistoric period the initial invasions were by Indo-
Europeans, who subsequently expanded their holdings
through colonization.[1]

Four principal components of the Greek peoples

came into the Aegean basin after 3000 B.C. The first of these were the Achaeans, who moved overland from the north and east shortly after 2000 B.C. to settle in the central Peloponnesus region, in Boeotia, Thessaly and the north-east Aegean. They were followed about 1500 B.C. by the Dorians, who moved into the eastern Peloponnesus, Crete, some of the south Aegean islands and the south-west corner of Asia Minor. Two subsequent groups of immigrants were the Ionians, who occupied Attica, the islands of the middle Aegean and the mainland of western Asia Minor from Miletus to Phocaea, and the Aetolians, who settled in parts of west central Greece, the northern Peloponnesus and some of the offshore islands. There appears to have been a considerable amount of overlapping of peoples and occupational areas in the second millennium B.C., and no doubt this accounted for the rivalry and political disunity which was to be an important element of later Greek history.

The precise relationship between the invading Indo-Europeans and the indigenous peoples of the Aegean basin, who, in addition to occupying many of the islands, lived on the mainland to the east and west, is difficult to determine. Archaeological discoveries indicate that the general cultural forms of the native inhabitants were more developed in many respects than those of the invading peoples and had points of contact with Egypt, Anatolia and Mesopotamia. This fact need not be particularly surprising, however, since during the period before the Amarna Age there was a meeting and synthesis of Egyptian, Mesopotamian, Canaanite, Anatolian and Aegean influences around the eastern Mediterranean which affected each constituent member in turn. From this confluence emerged the earliest traditions of Greece, no less than those of Israel and other eastern Mediterranean nations.[2]

In the same way the historical situation of the pre-

Amarna period can throw some light on the relationship between the Minoan culture of Crete and that of the Mycenaeans (c. 1600-1100 B.C.), who lived on the mainland in such places as Argos, Mycenae and early Athens. There is no doubt that the Mycenaeans had much more in common with the larger complex of Near Eastern culture from the third millennium B.C. than with the civilization of the later classical Greeks.[3] Any true understanding of Mycenaean civilization must, therefore, relate it to its position in the international framework of the eastern Mediterranean region and particularly to the culture which obtained during the second half of the second millennium B.C.

In this general connection, the literary discoveries at Ras Shamra (Ugarit) have given new dimensions to the growing evidence of the Minoan inscriptions to show that, until some time after 1500 B.C., Greece, Ugarit and Israel all belonged to the same cultural sphere. In this milieu the most important linguistic and cultural element, having regard to the varying and composite make-up of all the peoples involved, was Canaanite-Phoenician. This recognition will inevitably exert a profound effect upon current ideas of ancient history, the origins of the Hellenic peoples and the provenance of the Hebrew Bible—in other words, upon the very foundations of Western civilization.

Archaeological discoveries have shown that Ugarit was the heir of all the preceding great cultures, from the glories of Sumeria to the richness of Amarna Age Egypt. It also had the closest associations with such peoples as the Hittites and Hurrians, who were of prime importance during the Mycenaean era, but were destined to disappear from the pages of history and needed the activities of the archaeologist to revive the memory of their significance in ancient Near Eastern life and culture. Ugarit was, of course, connected intimately with the

Phoenicians, who were spreading eastern Mediterranean civilization wherever possible by means of their maritime trading activities. Most important of all, though it is certain that the ancients could hardly have realized it, was the fact that Ugarit was in contact with the precursors of the classical Greeks and Hebrews, the two peoples who were destined to become the founders of Western civilization by their combined and parallel achievements. All this is not to say, however, that the inhabitants of ancient Ugarit were neither talented nor enterprising in their own right. Nevertheless, it is true they were fortunate that their culture flourished during the Amarna Age, and that they were located at the crossroads of the Western world where the seeds of both Hellas and Israel had already been planted and were flourishing.

Historians and others have for too long been accustomed to make the tacit assumption that Israel and Greece were independent cultures which flourished in almost complete isolation from one another. While this is superficially so, to the extent that there was never any Parthenon in Palestine nor Moses in Hellas, it is now clear from the discoveries at Ras Shamra that the Ugaritic epics exhibit unmistakable and organic parallels of a kind which link the pre-prophetic Hebrews with the pre-philosophical Greeks.

It would thus appear that, in the second millennium B.C., the Greeks and Hebrews were members of the same international social and cultural order in the eastern Mediterranean. During the first millennium B.C. down to the eighth century B.C., the Greeks and Hebrews each produced their distinctive classical contributions to Near Eastern culture, but with the conquests of Alexander the Great in the fourth century B.C. both peoples were once again thrown together in the Hellenic pattern of life. While the Ugaritic epic compositions are closely related in both language and thought-forms to the Hebrew Old Testament, they also show an association with Aegean culture. Thus, through the Helen of Troy motif in the Epic of Keret, Ugaritic literature managed to bridge the gap between Genesis and the *Iliad*.

This type of interrelationship naturally has a bearing upon the origin of Minoan culture. Whereas the pre-Minoans of Crete are now known to have come from the mainland and from Anatolia, the Minoans themselves evidently migrated from a southern climate. This seems to be indicated by the way in which they consistently failed to provide some kind of central heating in their buildings and palaces. It appears most probable that they originally came from the Nile Delta region, since Cretan archaeology has yielded many artefacts which were imported from, or fashioned in imitation of, Egyptian articles of commerce. Such an origin for the Minoans would seem likely because of the way in which Minoan chronology is linked to Near Eastern history principally through Egyptian scarabs and other pharaonic inscriptions uncovered in the Cretan excavations. On this basis, the author of Genesis 10: 13-14 was correct in deriving the Cretans (called the "Philistines" and "Caphtorim") from Egypt.

The significant differences between Egyptian culture and that of Minoan Crete are due to the fact that classical Egyptian civilization was primarily the product of life in Upper Egypt. By contrast, however, Lower Egypt, which included the Delta region, was much more a part of the eastern Mediterranean world, and many of its peoples were Semites and other non-Egyptians. In a real sense, therefore, the Nile Delta area was the cradle of western civilization. From this region appear to have come the Minoans, who founded the first advanced culture of Europe, while later on there emerged the Hebrews of the Exodus period, who migrated to their

Promised Land and established the religious patterns which subsequently undergirded Western civilization. On such a basis, the precursors of the classical Greek and Hebrew cultures were, in fact, kindred Delta folk.

While Babylonia still exercised the dominant influence in the Amarna Age, her ability to exert military control over the Aegean had ceased with the termination of the First Dynasty of Babylon on the death of Hammurabi in the eighteenth century B.C. However, the benefits of Babylonian culture had already been absorbed by the Hurrians, Hittites, Phoenicians and others, and in the seventeenth and sixteenth centuries B.C. its dissemination was facilitated by the expansion of the Hyksos empire. During the Amarna Age proper, this role was taken over by the Egyptian New Kingdom after the expulsion of the Hyksos from Egypt, and through the Egyptians it persisted in the Levant.

This is the reason why the Homeric traditions do not mention such nations as Babylonia or Assyria, but instead concentrate attention upon the eastern Mediterranean cultures of Egypt, Syria, Phoenicia, Cyprus and various Anatolian centres, through which Mesopotamian influence persisted in the West. Nevertheless, it is still true, as Schliemann showed after he had excavated the grave circle at Mycenae in 1876, that the Mycenaeans were Greeks, whose nearest linguistic relatives in the Aegean were the Arcadians, who lived in the mountainous core of the peninsula, the Cypriots, who came within the Dorian linguistic group, and the Ionians.

Mycenaean civilization seems to have been a development of an earlier Minoan culture, traces of which were first uncovered by Sir Arthur Evans in 1900. Excavating at the ancient site of Knossos in Crete, Evans first found a number of inscribed tablets, then a huge complex of buildings which required many seasons of sustained digging to uncover. When the preliminary work had been accomplished, it became evident that ancient Knossos had formed the centre of a vigorous civilization which Evans named Minoan, after Minos, the legendary ruler of Crete.

This culture appears to have lasted for the better part of a millennium, beginning about 2000 B.C., although datable Egyptian artefacts unearthed at Knossos would suggest that the royal palace, at least, was destroyed about 1400 B.C. Like the Hyksos and the New Kingdom Egyptians, the Minoans used the horse-drawn chariot prominently in their military formations, though their chariots apparently did not carry the same heavy iron fittings as the Semitic vehicles, since the Tiryns fresco depicts two women driving in a chariot which was apparently engaged in hunting.[4] Minoan art and architecture had a good deal in common with that which obtained on the Greek mainland, while Minoan pottery styles, which emerged over various generations, set ceramic fashions throughout the ancient Near East. The recognition that specific sequences of this kind actually occurred made possible a system of ceramic dating in archaeological excavations, a technique which has proved of inestimable value since its discovery.

Of particular interest were the tablets recovered from Knossos, the capital of a legendary empire in Homeric tradition. The largest body of texts, known as Linear B, comprised about 4,000 tablets, some of which were recovered from sites on the Greek mainland. A much smaller group, Linear A, comprised about 150 economic and administrative tablets written in a script quite similar to that of the Linear B tablets. The Minoan system of writing exhibited recognizable continuity, beginning with the Cretan hieroglyphs and carrying on through the various forms of Linear A and B tablets and the Cypro-Minoan down to the Cypride texts which came from the third century B.C.

A great deal of scholarly discussion and argument preceded the successful attempts by Michael Ventris to assign sufficient correct values to the Linear B syllabary to establish the basis for reading the tablets.[5] The economic and administrative texts of this character were published in 1956,[6] and were shown to be essentially Greek in nature and to have had affinities with the traditions of other eastern Mediterranean lands, particularly with the culture of Mesopotamia.

The language of Linear A has not been determined satisfactorily at the time of writing. Some scholars have maintained that Linear A contains an Indo-European language, which may possibly have affinities with Hittite and other languages and dialects in use in early Anatolia. C. H. Gordon, however, has taken the view that it is basically Semitic in nature and closely related to Babylonian Akkadian.[7]

About 1400 B.C. Greek invaders sacked Knossos, the cultural centre of the Minoan civilization, and scattered the survivors throughout the Aegean. Some of them attempted to settle in Egypt in the New Kingdom period, but they were driven away in a naval battle with Ramses III and ultimately settled in the Gaza region of Palestine, as mentioned previously. About 1200 B.C. a Greek expedition conquered the famous city of Ilium or Troy, celebrated in Homeric tradition. At the same time, another group of Indo-Europeans swept down into the Greek peninsula. Meeting with local resistance, however, they turned away and attacked central and eastern Asia Minor, bringing about the downfall of the Hittite empire. It is quite possible also that at this period the Etruscans were forced to leave Lydia in south-western Asia Minor and to migrate westwards, ultimately settling in Italy north of the River Tiber.

After some time the Greek invaders absorbed the remnants of the earlier cultures which had flourished on the mainland and made the Greek language, in its various dialects, the spoken tongue of the Hellenic world. Out of necessity they developed maritime skills, eventually surpassing even the Phoenicians in this area of activity. During the Age of the Kings (c. 1000-750 B.C.) the various cities which were established constituted autonomous states, and the degree of respect which each of them demanded for their political and economic rights led ultimately to friction, suspicion and national disunity. The tenth to the eighth centuries B.C. saw a period of colonization, in which such distant places as southern Italy, Corsica, Spain, North Africa and the Nile Delta were settled by Greek elements. While this movement resulted in the dissemination of Greek religious, intellectual and cultural traditions throughout the Mediterranean area, it also perpetuated the feuds and narrow suspicions of the homeland, with the result that, in the end, the political influence of Greek colonization was nullified.[8]

The culture of the age was enshrined in the celebrated *Iliad* and *Odyssey* of Homer, written most probably between 800 and 700 B.C. These compositions, like the heroic narratives from a later period of northern Europe, dealt with such popular topics as the exploits of heroes, adventures at sea and in foreign lands, the conquest of cities such as Troy and other themes which readily lent themselves to epic treatment. As Gordon has pointed out,[9] the traditions of the Greek Heroic Age have many points of contact with the contemporary Semitic cultures of the Near East.

The earlier Greek kings were ultimately displaced by the rise of an aristocratic class, a process which may have been hastened, if not actually initiated, by the Dorian invasion. This situation was reflected in the writings of Homer, from which it is clear that the kings of the Greek city-states were already less powerful than the rulers of

Mycenae or Knossos had been. While the decay of monarchy was not by any means uniform throughout the Hellenic world, it seems certain that by 650 B.C. kingship had virtually disappeared in Greece.

A new series of social problems occurred with the introduction of coined money, the beginnings of which are generally attributed to the fabulously wealthy king Croesus of Lydia in the sixth century B.C. Rich land-owners could now convert a portion of their wealth into money, whereas the poor peasants still depended to a large extent upon the barter of their agricultural pro-duce. When harvests were poor or failed entirely, they had no choice but to pledge either their lands or them-selves, if they did not own the land which they worked, as security for payment in the future.

Added to this unfortunate situation was the threat imposed by slave-labour imported from abroad, which invariably weighed heavily against the poor peasants and in favour of the wealthy landowners. Some relief was obtained in 621 B.C., due in no small measure to the political insight and insistence of Solon of Athens. In 594 B.C. this man was given the authority to redress the imbalance of the economy of Attica, a task which he undertook with considerable skill. Perhaps the most significant aspect of his entire legislative programme was the principle by which property, rather than noble birth, became the qualification for admission to high political office.

Solon is generally credited with having divided up contemporary Greek society into four classes, on the basis of which he instituted what can well be called a moderate oligarchy. The particular class to which an individual could be assigned was related as much to the productivity of the land which he possessed as to its actual size. This procedure was consistent with the econ-omic policies of Solon, which aimed at encouraging manufacture and trade, especially the exporting of olive-oil, in which Athens was rich. The success of his commercial legislation may be judged from the fact that it was chiefly responsible for laying the foundation upon which the future economic greatness of Athens was constructed.

The land reforms which Solon instituted laid great stress upon the ability of the individual to work in freedom, and the virtue of private enterprise. Accordingly Solon began a programme of emancipation under which those persons who had been obliged to become slaves because of a crushing burden of debt were restored to freedom. In a further move, aimed at enhancing individual self-respect and enterprise, he abolished the old Attic legislation relating to debtors, under which a person who owed money was permitted to present his own person as security.

Probably the most important of the changes which established the reputation of Solon as a statesman was the institution of the courts of justice in Athens. With true democratic insight, Solon transferred the sovereign power from the magistrates and the areopagus, and placed it within the jurisdiction of the citizenry. In cases of actual trials, legislation was passed whereby the jury was appointed from the body of the citizens by lot. These two developments contained the germ of a vigorous democratic growth which was to come to full flower in the age of Pericles.

By about 600 B.C. even the influence of the rich and powerful nobles had diminished, and shortly thereafter it began to be replaced by that of local "tyrants". These men were political opportunists who employed force or trickery as a means of seizing power in the city-states and administering them for their own benefit. The designation "tyrant" had originally been borrowed from monarchical Lydia, and had existed before 600

B.C. at Corinth, Megara and Miletus. When Solon was still a young man, an attempt had been made at Athens to introduce the rule of tyrants, but this had been thwarted.

By the seventh century B.C. a capitalist class had arisen as a consequence of the vast expansion of trade and commerce in Greece, and this situation provoked resentment among the already downtrodden peasants. Against this background of middle-class capitalism and lower-class poverty, there arose the Age of Democracy in Greece in the sixth century B.C. The demand for self-rule along democratic lines led to the formulation of legislation designed to limit the power of individuals, but, though this procedure bore some fruit in Athens under Cleisthenes, it encountered only limited success elsewhere.

But in another area, that of religion, the rise of Greek law witnessed the substitution of loftier ethical ideals for the crude anthropomorphisms of an earlier era, in which the Olympian deities had been endowed with attributes which did not reflect particularly creditably upon their human creators. Significant developments also occurred in agrarian reform, philosophy, music and physical science, for which such eminent thinkers as Thales, Pythagoras, Xenophanes, Heracleitus, Anaximander and others were responsible. The Ionian coast of Asia Minor, rather than Attica or the Peloponnesus, seems to have been the cultural centre during this period in the growth of Greek thought.

Speculative philosophy and republican government, the two institutions which became the hallmark of later Hellenism, had scarcely gained a firm foothold in Greece when the country was confronted with a crisis of unprecedented proportions. The rise of Cyrus of Media brought with it the westward expansion of the Medo-Persian empire into Anatolia, and once Cambyses, son of Cyrus, had conquered Egypt in 525 B.C. the Persians exerted control over western Asia as far as the Aegean and the Hellespont. These territorial holdings were soon supplemented by the addition of the western shore of the Black Sea and the north coast of the Aegean, as well as by the conquest of Cyrenaica to the west of Egypt.

To some extent this rapid expansion had been aided unwittingly by generations of Greek mercenary soldiers, who had constituted an important segment of the Babylonian armies and had subsequently fought for the Persians alongside units mustered from nations west of the River Euphrates. In point of fact, attestable Greek influence in the Near East is surprisingly early, as is made evident by the presence of mid-seventh century B.C. Greek colonies in Egypt at Naucratis and Tahpanhes, and by the use of Greek mercenaries in the Egyptian and Babylonian armies at the Battle of Carchemish in 605 B.C.

Cyrus II followed the Babylonian tradition of showing tolerance towards captive peoples, but went a step further in gaining goodwill for his regime by liberating those national groups which Nebuchadnezzar II had carried captive. The Cyrus Cylinder recorded the edict which permitted all expatriates to return to their homeland[10] and this material, along with the Aramaic edicts in the Book of Ezra[11] and the Elephantine papyri,[12] indicates that the Persian rulers took a genuine interest in the religious and social welfare of their subjects.

Cyrus II was killed in 530 B.C. during a battle with militant groups in the north-eastern hills of Persia and was succeeded by his son Cambyses II (530-522 B.C.), who had already been acting as co-regent. Cambyses, who had brought Egypt into the Persian empire by defeating Psamtik III at Pelusium in 525 B.C., became mentally deranged shortly after the death of his father and committed suicide in 522 B.C. His death was the signal for the outbreak of revolts in some of the outlying provinces, but order was finally restored by Darius I (522-486 B.C.) in 522 B.C. The new monarch was the son of Hystaspes, and ruled over both Persia and Babylon.

In the west, Darius secured Persian control over Asia Minor by adding the neighbouring islands to a subjugated Ionia. But, instead of launching a military campaign against the Peisistratids of Athens, Darius undertook an expedition against the troublesome Scythians in the area of the Black and Caspian seas,[13] and for a time the Greek mainland was relieved of the threat of Persian occupation. Ionia, however, soon became the scene of one of the first conflicts with Persia when a revolt occurred there in 499 B.C. This affair terminated in a sea battle at Lade in 494 B.C., in which the courage of the Chians and Milesians proved unequal to the treachery of Greek contingents from Samos and Lesbos, and to the might of the Persian army.

A more successful resistance to Persian forces took place in 490 B.C., when a naval expedition under Darius I sailed into the straits between Euboea and Attica and landed at the Bay of Marathon. The Athenians hurriedly summoned aid from Sparta and, though greatly outnumbered, decided to make a stand against the Persians at Marathon. The Greek general Miltiades, who had first-hand experience of Persian military tactics, led a flanking movement which resulted in the Persian archers being overwhelmed by the Greek phalanx of hoplites.

Although heavily defeated, the Persians were determined to subjugate the mainland and establish their authority in the Peloponnese. The Greeks, for their part, set aside their petty differences and suspicions in order to prepare for a renewed attack by the Persians. Themistocles laid great emphasis upon the necessity for assembling strong naval forces, but, although an appeal was addressed to the whole of Greece, only Athens and Sparta made serious preparations for the coming onslaught. Under Xerxes I (486-464 B.C.) the Persians again attacked Greece, launching their campaign in 480 B.C. in a co-ordinated movement of land and sea forces. The Spartan king, Leonidas, tried to halt the Persian army at the pass of Thermopylae, some ninety miles north-west of Athens, but he was betrayed and killed in an historic battle.

A part of the Persian fleet which had been sent around Euboea to attack the Athenian ships from the rear was destroyed in a storm, but the remaining naval units trapped the Greek fleet securely in the Bay of Salamis. When the Persians set fire to Athens, the Greek ships broke out in desperation and in the battle which followed inflicted shattering losses on the Persian fleet. Xerxes hastily withdrew his forces northwards across the Hellespont and marched back to Persia, leaving a small military detachment to attack Attica the following year. This Persian expedition gained some small initial successes, but it was repulsed with heavy losses by the Spartan general Pausanias at the Battle of Plataea in 479 B.C. So serious was this defeat that, had it not been for the prompt action of the Persian cavalry, the expeditionary force would have been wiped out to a man. As it was, Mardonius, the Persian commander who had gained an easy victory in Attica, was killed at Plataea.

To forestall the possibility of future Persian invasions, the Greek states entered into a political alliance known as the Delian League, which had as a primary responsibility the maintaining of adequate naval defensive forces. It comprised the cities of Euboea, the colonies of the northern Aegean, the islanders, the Ionians and the Greek city-states of Asia Minor. Athens contributed the majority of the ships, with the islands of Lesbos, Chios and Samos making up the balance, and the other members of the League paid an annual quota of money. Under the leadership of Cimon, son of Miltiades of Athens, the League presented an imposing obstacle to any lingering Persian military and territorial ambitions in the Aegean.

While this confederacy afforded proper opportunities for participation by all its members, it contained within itself the seeds of political dissension, if only because it was a voluntary association of states upon which a subsequent Athenian empire was constructed with little or no regard to the feelings of the members. Most of the participants in this maritime league were far from wealthy and, although the basis of the association involved each state furnishing ships to the common fleet, many could do no more than supply one vessel, or even part of a vessel. Dissatisfaction on the latter score was avoided by the proviso that the smaller states should contribute an annual sum of money to a common treasury instead of providing ships. Thus, almost from the start, the League consisted of two classes of members: those who provided the ships, such as the Athenians, and those who made a comparable contribution in money. Determining the amount of the latter in individual cases was by no means an easy task, and it is to the credit of Aristides that the scale of valuation which he instituted for those states unable to contribute vessels remained in force for more than half a century.

The council of the League met at Delos, where the treasury was located, and all members were accorded an equal vote in the proceedings. This situation, however, was less democratic than might have appeared at first sight, since the Athenians were readily able to influence the smaller states and accumulate votes for their own policies. In any event, as leaders of the League, the Athenians in effect wielded executive power and, whether the associated states liked it or not, Athens was in control of a situation which enabled her to begin the gradual transformation of the maritime league into a naval empire.

Xerxes I was assassinated in 464 B.C. and was succeeded by his son Artaxerxes I Longimanus (464-425 B.C.), who in general endeavoured to follow the administrative policies which had been laid down by his father. The latter, unfortunately, had failed to commend himself to the Egyptians because he had suppressed with unusual brutality a revolt which had broken out in Egypt after the death of Darius I. The situation deteriorated further in 466 B.C. when a Phoenician fleet under Persian command sailed into the Aegean and was destroyed, along with accompanying land forces, by Cimon and his League forces near the mouth of the River Eurymedon. This demonstration of Persian weakness encouraged further revolts in Egypt in 460 B.C., and these continued until about 454 B.C. when Persia reasserted its authority in the eastern Mediterranean.

In considerable alarm, the Greeks transferred the headquarters of the League from Delos to Athens, thus asserting the supremacy of the latter and making particularly clear her political and military independence of Sparta. An Athenian empire was built up rapidly, and under the leadership of Pericles the city of Athens far surpassed all her previous glory.[14] The achievements of this era found permanent record in such magnificent structures as the buildings on the Acropolis, particularly the Parthenon. Unfortunately, the administration of Pericles witnessed the outbreak of war between Athens and Sparta in 459 B.C., and a series of battles took place in the Peloponnesus. While these were in progress, Pericles decided to make peace with Artaxerxes I, and in 448 B.C. concluded a treaty with the Persians in order to avoid the prospect of a war on two fronts. Shortly

PLATE 9. The Ishtar Gate of Babylon. A painting by Maurice Bardin of the reconstruction according to Unger of the city of Babylon. The Ishtar Gate is in the foreground, with the "Hanging Gardens" and the Great Ziggurat in the upper right.

(*By courtesy of the Oriental Institute, University of Chicago.*)

PLATE 10. The Rosetta Stone. Discovered in 1799 by Napoleon's
engineers in Egypt, the trilingual inscription in old hieroglyphic,
demotic Egyptian and Greek led to the decipherment of ancient
Egyptian.

(*By courtesy of the Trustees of the British Museum.*)

after this time, Athens suffered several reverses, including the loss of Boeotia in 447 B.C., and a humiliating peace with the Peloponnesians was concluded the following year.

This situation brought the leadership which Pericles had furnished into serious question. From the beginning, he had been strongly imperialistic in his policies, and it had been his avowed intention to increase the physical dimensions of the Athenian empire as well as to extend the political influence of Athens within the borders of Greece as a whole.

However, the recent conflicts, which had included the failure of an Athenian naval expedition to Egypt in 456 B.C., had imposed a serious strain upon the economic resources of Athens. This situation, combined with the realization which the terms of the Thirty Years' Peace (446 B.C.) brought to the Athenians that future hopes of conquest must be related to a maritime rather than a land empire, posed a serious threat to the position of Pericles.

Perhaps the most significant challenge came from the oligarchical party at Athens, which had increased in influence as the fortunes of the country diminished. The members of this group took exception to the state of democratic procedures in Athens, and also attacked the imperialist ambitions of Pericles as a matter of political principle.

A more honest champion of the cause of those cities comprising the original Delian alliance which Athens had by now built up into an empire was Thucydides, the son of Melesias. He was openly critical of the way in which the tribute imposed by Athens upon the confederate states had frequently been spent either on the imperial city itself or on objectives which were of little or no real benefit to the member states.

In effect, Thucydides maintained that the tribute

E

ought to have been reserved exclusively for the purpose entertained at the time of the original levy, namely the defence of Greece against Persia. Instead of this, he urged, the funds available had actually been dissipated on an Athenian military campaign in Boeotia.

A lesser man than Pericles might have succumbed to the political implications involving the alleged mismanagement of public funds. Instead, he routed the opposing forces by introducing an avowedly imperialistic policy which, in the event, became so popular at Athens that it stifled further criticism of his empire-building. The most important element of this policy was the system which he devised of settling Athenian citizens in different parts of the empire. This procedure achieved the twofold objective of relieving the pressure of population in overcrowded Athens and ensuring that the more distant reaches of subject allies were garrisoned by troops loyal to Athens.

But in his attempt to make his capital city pre-eminent in all Greece, Pericles again fell under suspicion of corruption. The occasion was the restoration of the temples in Athens, which had suffered considerably from the effects of the war with the Persians. Pericles began the restoration of these structures on a grand scale, giving as his reason the fact that Athens was bound, in sacred duty, to discharge her debt to the gods in this manner for the defeat of the Medes. Once again, Thucydides led the outcry which accused Pericles of mismanaging money given to Athens for specific purposes.

On this occasion, however, there does seem to have been less fact and more political sophistry in Thucydides' attack. While it was true that a small amount of money had been taken from the common treasury, the bulk of the expense involved in the rebuilding programme was borne by the Athenians themselves. Thucydides attempted to bring the matter to a head in 442 B.C., but he was no match for the popular Pericles, and in the end the people voted for the ostracism of Thucydides. By this act they demonstrated their approval for the policies of Pericles and, at the same time, removed his most influential and vocal opponent.

Hostilities again broke out in 431 B.C. in a struggle known as the Peloponnesian War (431-404 B.C.), the principal theme of the historical writings of Thucydides. Sparta and her Peloponnesian allies were once more confronted by the superior economic and military resources of Athens, and the conflict was precipitated by the Theban attack on Plataea in 431 B.C., which was followed by the first invasion of Attica in 430 B.C. Pericles died in 429 B.C., the year in which Plataea was besieged by the Spartans and captured after two years of resistance. Demosthenes, the Athenian general, campaigned with the Greek fleet off the western Peloponnese and succeeded in isolating some Spartan troops on the island of Sphacteria. These limited successes, however, were offset by Athenian failures in Boeotia and Thrace, and a peace was ultimately negotiated by Nicias with Sparta in 421 B.C.

Darius II (423-404 B.C.), the son and successor of Artaxerxes I, was able to capitalize upon the earlier phases of the Peloponnesian War, one result of which was that Sparta issued an urgent appeal for Persian help against Athens. This turn of events meant that the position of Darius II in the western part of his empire was strengthened considerably, and when the Athenians mounted a disastrous expedition against Sicily in 413 B.C the opportunity was provided for Tissaphernes, a powerful and unscrupulous Persian diplomat, to reoccupy Lydia.[15]

Unfortunately, the political advantage which Darius II had gained from the events in Greece was largely nullified as the result of court intrigues in Persia, and it was not long before Tissaphernes himself was relieved of his position. The young Persian prince Cyrus journeyed westward to witness the end of the struggle between Athens and Sparta, and became a friend of Lysander, the leader of the Spartan troops. Lysander won a decisive victory over the Athenians at Aegospotami, and in 404 B.C. the Athenians capitulated to Sparta, thus terminating the war. Order was restored in Athens by the Rule of the Thirty in 404 B.C., but Spartan hegemony was repudiated the following year. Socrates, the philosopher and mentor of Plato, was made the scapegoat for past failures and put to death in 399 B.C.

In the meantime, Artaxerxes II (404-359 B.C.), son of Darius II and grandson of Artaxerxes I, had succeeded to the Persian throne, having crushed the rebellion of his brother Cyrus at the Battle of Cunaxa in 401 B.C., as described by Xenophon in his *Anabasis*. The Egyptians of the Delta region revolted against the Persians in 405 B.C., and even the Jewish mercenaries at the Nile military colony of Elephantine were compelled to transfer their allegiance from Persia to Egypt, a situation which Artaxerxes was unable to remedy.

From 397 B.C. the victorious Spartans under Lysander showed an increasing interest in the political affairs of Asia Minor, but their expansionist ambitions were thwarted by the Peace of Antalcidas in 386 B.C., in which Artaxerxes II reasserted his claim to Asia Minor. The Spartans then turned their attention to their more immediate neighbours, but an attack upon Thebes and Athens resulted in a lengthy war, from which the Theban forces under Epaminondas emerged victorious at the Battle of Leuctra in 371 B.C. Whereupon the Thebans, who were favourably disposed towards the Persian regime, determined to end Spartan supremacy, and with his allies Epaminondas marched into the

Peloponnese, only to be defeated at Mantinea in 362 B.C. Despite the victory, Sparta never recovered her earlier predominance, whereas Athens suddenly found herself in the middle of a commercial revival which soon made her the foremost trading centre in Greece.

The last years of Artaxerxes II were marked by revolts and the internal weaknesses of the Achaemenid regime began to become apparent. Artaxerxes died in 359 B.C. and was succeeded by his son Artaxerxes III Ochus (359-338 B.C.), reputedly the most bloodthirsty of all the Achaemenid rulers. He suppressed the revolt of the Cadusians, who lived near the Hyrcanian Sea, and absorbed their troops into his armies as mercenaries. The Athenians took advantage of growing resentment against the Persians to stir up revolt in Asia Minor, but were persuaded by Demosthenes not to embark upon a full-scale war with the Persians. In 354 B.C. a peace was negotiated, in which Athens lost control of her former island empire. Once affairs in the Aegean had been satisfactorily concluded from the Persian standpoint, Artaxerxes III set about the reconquest of Egypt. He encountered determined opposition under Nectanebo II (359-341 B.C.), however, and had to withdraw his forces in 350 B.C.

The accession year of Artaxerxes III was significant in that it witnessed the rise to power of Philip of Macedon, a talented leader whose ambition it was firstly to make Macedonia the most powerful area of Greece and then to conquer the entire country itself. The hill-tribes of Macedonia were subjugated in 358 B.C., and in the same year Philip gained control of the Athenian colony of Amphipolis, where he built the city of Philippi. Five years later he attacked the Thracian coast and invaded Thessaly, but was subsequently repulsed by Phocian mercenaries, who were themselves defeated by Philip in 352 B.C.

For eight years he campaigned in the Balkan highlands, but in 349 B.C. attacked Olynthus, which fell two years later. Athens made peace overtures to Philip in 346 B.C., and this enabled him to turn his attention once more to the Balkan hill-country. Philip suffered a setback when his allies in Propontis revolted and the Athenians offered them their support, and his prestige further declined when sieges against Perinthus and Byzantium failed in 339 B.C. The following year, however, Philip marched into central Greece and won a decisive victory over his Peloponnesian opponents at Chaeroneia. In 337 B.C. he organized the Greek states into an Hellenic League, which he hoped to turn into a military force in readiness for an attack upon the Persians. An advance unit was sent into Asia in 336 B.C., but that year Philip was murdered in Macedonia.[16] The task of conquest therefore passed on to his son Alexander the Great (356-323 B.C.), a pupil of the Greek philosopher Aristotle.

Two years previously, Artaxerxes III had been poisoned by order of Bagoas, an imperial official, and the chaos which resulted raised Greek hopes of an early conquest of the Persian empire. But in 336 B.C. Darius III (336-330 B.C.) succeeded to the throne and immediately attempted to quell the unrest in his kingdom. He launched an expedition against Egypt, occupied the Nile Delta region after a naval battle and was recognized as king of Egypt in 334 B.C.

The policy of Darius III with regard to Egypt was not so much an attempt to reassert the authority of imperial Persia as to suppress the political ambitions of local satraps and to placate the populace of Egypt as a whole. This latter consideration was of particular importance in view of the way in which Artaxerxes III Ochus had ridden roughshod over the religious susceptibilities of the Egyptians by drowning the sacred bull Apis in the

Nile and instituting the ass as the sacred animal of Egyptian cult-worship. Because he did not engender serious political disenchantment with Persian rule, Darius III managed to regain a significant amount of Egyptian goodwill, even though he was weak in personality and far from being a forceful leader.

At this time, Alexander was bringing the tribes on the northern borders of Greece under his control and thus presented no immediate military threat to the Persians. Having conquered Egypt, Darius III returned to Persepolis and ignored a request from Athens for financial aid against Alexander until it became obvious that the latter intended to lead the Hellenic League organized by Philip against the Persians.

This movement began innocently enough in 334 B.C. with the conquest of Asia Minor, an event which revealed fully the essential weakness of Persian military resistance. The simple fact was that the Persians had fallen far behind in the art of waging war. They had not troubled to keep abreast of the military developments which had been taking place in Greece during the preceding half-century and in consequence had little appreciation of Greek abilities in this area. To make the situation even worse, this deficiency was coupled with a complete lack of understanding of Greek national and political aspirations. The Persians had come to rely too heavily upon their Greek mercenary troops and, with typical Mesopotamian conservatism, had not even troubled to ascertain whether or not new methods of encountering enemy tactics on the field of battle ought to be instituted.

The Persians, even more than the Babylonians, inclined strongly to defensive procedures in battle, trusting in the weight of their chariotry and the bravery of their troops to bring about the desired victory. All that a potential enemy needed was the knowledge that the Persians were wholly incapable of shaping offensive strategic plans. Therefore, even the slightest departure from conventional means of waging war would be sufficient to place the Persian forces at an important psychological and tactical disadvantage and force them to the brink of defeat.

Alexander realized that, for the first time, apart from a few picked units and a body of Greek mercenaries, the king of Persia had no first-quality troops whatsoever in his armies. Added to this situation was the fact that Darius himself was a poor leader, who maintained, at best, a rather tenuous hold over unreliable satraps. Alexander won a decisive victory over the Persians at Issus in 333 B.C. But, instead of pursuing the enemy, he chose to consolidate his southern flank by marching through Syria and Palestine to Egypt, where he was regarded as a liberator. So relieved were the Egyptians to exchange the overlordship of Persia for that of Greece that they accepted Alexander as a legitimate pharaoh[17] and afforded him facilities for the construction of the city of Alexandria.

In 331 B.C. Alexander marched north and east, crossing the Upper Tigris near Arbela. Here he inflicted another decisive defeat upon Darius, who was murdered after the battle by two of his own followers. Babylon, Susa and Persepolis fell quickly into Greek hands, and it was not long before Alexander began to assume the character of an oriental despot. Pushing eastwards in 329 B.C., he marched through Afghanistan and conquered Bactria and Sogdiana. He paused at Samarcand, capital of Sogdiana, to marry an oriental princess and then pressed on through the Hindu Kush to the Punjab.

Whatever plans Alexander may have had for leading his troops further east were, however, thwarted when his soldiers flatly refused to follow, and despite threats and cajoling he was compelled to lead them back to Babylon. Nevertheless, his fame as a conqueror had spread throughout the entire East, and ambassadors from distant points of the old Persian empire were beginning to arrive in Babylon, anxious to obtain the goodwill of the new monarch who now ruled over the largest empire known to man. But Alexander had barely commenced the Hellenizing of his newly won domain when, weakened by the rigours of his campaigns, he caught a fever and died in 323 B.C. in the prime of life.

CHAPTER 6

The Hellenic Empire and Rome

The conquests of Alexander had opened the entire East to the infiltration of Western ideas and, although no longer able to give imperial leadership, for the next three centuries Greece contributed its civilization to what has become known as the Hellenic Age. The virility of this culture was due in no small measure to the influence of Aristotle, a pupil of Plato, who explored with great thoroughness the intellectual and phenomenal realms.[1] He began his investigations from the methodological standpoint of a logician, but as his studies expanded into the field of biology he developed more scientific techniques. A man of immense erudition, he exercised an enormous influence over science and philosophy alike for many centuries. After his death, there was a decline in scientific study in Athens, but interest in this area of enquiry was kindled in Alexandria, where it flourished under the patronage of the Ptolemaic rulers of Egypt.

One feature of Alexandrian study was the collection and application of the medical theories of Hippocrates, who in the late fifth century B.C. had founded a medical academy on the island of Cos. As a result, Alexandria became the leading medical centre of the Mediterranean world and was particularly renowned for the way in which post-mortem studies of the human body were fostered. The Alexandrians also achieved notable successes in the field of literature, though much of their work proved to be a rather slavish imitation of the master-pieces issuing from the Classical period of Greek literature. The purity of the language employed in these writings contrasted sharply with the colloquial Greek spoken throughout the eastern Mediterranean, and the work of such authors as Callimachus and Theocritus betrayed little hint of the contamination of Greek by extraneous syntactical forms and borrowed words such as can be found, for example, in the New Testament writings.

Two important products of the world which Alexander the Great had created were the philosophical approaches to life of Zeno and Epicurus. The former, who lived from about 336 to 264 B.C., was of Phoenician origin, and some scholars have attributed the moral rigour of his character and general tenets to his Semitic background. In denying the possibility of free will, Zeno, the founder of Stoicism, embraced a determinist, or perhaps fatalist, philosophy. With Socrates, Plato and Aristotle, the Stoics adopted a thoroughgoing teleology, believing that the world had been constructed by a perfect and beneficent creator so as to secure the greatest good of mankind. They also used the Greek term *logos* (word) to describe a principle of rationality permeating all of nature which, despite their philosophical monism, had overtones of pantheism. Stoic doctrine conceded some form of human survival after death, but it was only held to last until the end of the particular world-period to which it belonged; after that it would be absorbed into the divine essence in preparation for a new creative phase.

The teachings of Epicurus (342-270 B.C.) had their roots in the natural philosophy taught in the schools of Asia Minor, but accommodated the emphasis upon the pursuit of happiness as found in the philosophies of such notable Athenians as Plato. Epicurus reacted against the

gross superstition of his age by rejecting all super-
naturalist beliefs and denying the possibility of human
survival after death. This was not so much the espousal
of atheism as the declaration that, in fact, the immortal
deities paid no heed whatsoever to mundane affairs,
being themselves glorified Epicureans. Happiness, therefore, was the predominant aim in life, and this, trans-
lated into practical terms, meant that pleasure was the
one true good. Such pleasure was of an intellectual
rather than a sensuous nature and, in the sense that
escape from the evils and ills of life was an important
goal of attainment, was passive rather than active.
Those who took this philosophy seriously lived exemplary
lives and, though its influence in the Hellenic world
was rather limited, it met the needs of men and women
who preferred to retreat into amiable self-gratification
rather than face up to the problems of everyday
living.

By far the weakest of all the areas of Hellenic culture
was the religious sphere. Although the crude anthropo-
morphic deities of Olympus were passing into eclipse,
due in no small measure to the enquiries of science and
philosophy, the spirit of superstition still persisted in the
influence exerted by the mystery religions. These forms
of worship became popular because of a pronounced
desire in the third century B.C. for a personal religion,
and this movement was encouraged by the attempts of
Alexander the Great at religious syncretism. The
mystery religions aimed at raising the soul above the
level of perishable matter to immortal life through
actual union with the divine, and functioned at an
intensely emotional and personal level.

It is important to observe that the "soul" as under-
stood by the majority of the mystery religions was the
Greek characterization of an emotional-metaphysical
entity thought to be imprisoned in the body and set free

only by the death of the individual. By contrast with the purity of the "soul", the body was regarded as basically evil in nature, thus stifling the creative forces inherent in the "soul". This concept is very different from that of the Hebrew *nephesh* or personality, which did not draw an artificial distinction between the physical and the metaphysical aspects of individual existence, but considered man as an integrated personality.

The cults of Cybele and Attis, which were diffused throughout Asia Minor, resembled the ancient Greek cult of Dionysius in some respects, while another popular religion was that of the Serapis, Isis and Osiris devotees. This was a syncretistic cult which had been created by Ptolemy the Great in order to unite the Greeks and Egyptians in his domain, and it proved particularly attractive to the less cultured Greek classes of freedmen and slaves. Of the oriental religions, the worship of Mithra, a Persian deity who can well be regarded as the inspiration for later Zoroastrianism, became widespread in the eastern Mediterranean and Europe because of its emphasis upon brotherhood, reconciliation and strict moral discipline. A development of the older Dionysius cult with the incorporation of the frenzied Bacchanal rites was seen in Orphism, which included among its tenets a theology of redemption, original sin and a cycle of reincarnation.

Though all these religions were in evidence across the Hellenic world, the third century B.C. was still one of spiritual turmoil and upheaval, with men looking everywhere for a fresh, personal vision of God. These conditions resulted to some extent from Alexander the Great's untimely death in 323 B.C., an occurrence which shocked the ancient world and left Greece bereft of leadership at the height of her political power. In an attempt to solve the impasse so dramatically created by his demise, the generals of Alexander decided to divide up the conquered territories of the Near East among themselves, which resulted in the formation of five separate provinces. Egypt was placed under the control of Ptolemy, who served as regent for a time before becoming supreme ruler, while Babylonia formed the seat of the Seleucid regime. Macedonia was allotted to Antipater, while Thrace and Phrygia were governed by Lysimachus and Antigonus respectively. Subsequently, further divisions took place within the empire, and ultimately there emerged the three dynasties of Egypt, Syria and Macedonia.

The Ptolemaic Dynasty lasted for almost three centuries,[2] being given a firm political basis by Ptolemy I Soter (323-283 B.C.), who in 320 B.C. invaded and annexed Syria, after which he gained military control over Judea. But when Antigonus, the Seleucid ruler of Asia, opposed his military ambitions, Ptolemy decided to withdraw to his own land. Under his regime many Jews came to Alexandria as prisoners of war in 320 B.C., or as immigrants, and were employed in a mercenary capacity.

In 312 B.C. Ptolemy defeated Demetrius of Syria, the son of Antigonus, and again occupied Coele-Syria. The following year, however, he established a non-aggression pact with Demetrius. A third occupation of Syrian territory occurred in 301 B.C., the primary aim being the ultimate control of Judea—an issue which was settled in favour of Ptolemy at the Battle of Ipsus that same year.[3] The loyalty of Judea to Egypt was of continuing interest to the Ptolemaic Dynasty, whose members cultivated the friendship of the Jews. Ptolemy II (285-246 B.C.) was important because of the attention which he paid to Jewish history and culture in an attempt to maintain the affection of his Jewish subjects. During his reign the task of translating the Hebrew Scriptures into Greek was begun, and the resultant version was known as the

Septuagint, a name derived from the seventy scholars traditionally supposed to have been engaged in the task of translation.

The early Seleucids of Syria also showed a desire to cultivate the friendship of the Jews. Nicator, who had inherited a large portion of Babylonia and Syria on the death of Alexander, encouraged the Jews to migrate to Asia Minor by offering them grants of land and the privileges of citizenship. After the Battle of Ipsus, Seleucus I Nicator recovered territory in Syria and consolidated his hold on Asia Minor. Several important centres of Greek culture, including Laodicea, Antioch, Edessa, Beroea and Seleucia, were founded during his reign, which came to an untimely end in 282 B.C. when he was killed in the process of attempting to gain control of the entire empire of Alexander. The successors of Nicator in the Syrian regime, which lasted until 64 B.C., were not so tolerant towards the Jews and many of the tribulations of the latter, as recorded in such Jewish histories as I and II Maccabees, were due to Seleucid tyranny.

Seleucus II Callinicus (246-226 B.C.), son of Antiochus II of Syria, fought the Third Syrian (Laodicean) War against Ptolemy III Euergetes (247-221 B.C.) of Egypt, who had invaded Syria and was attempting to capture Seleucia. The resistance of Seleucus II proved futile, and when his forces were routed most of the Seleucid empire fell under Egyptian control. His son and successor Seleucus III Soter (226-223 B.C.) did not come into open conflict with Egypt until 223 B.C., when he attempted to reoccupy parts of Asia Minor and was killed in battle. Ptolemy III was murdered in 221 B.C. by his son and successor Ptolemy IV Philopator (221-203 B.C.), under whom the Ptolemaic Dynasty began to decline.[4] In 220 B.C. Antiochus III of Syria (223-187 B.C.), the successor of Seleucus III, invaded Coele-Syria, but was defeated by the Egyptians in 217 B.C. during a battle at Raphia. He then marched eastwards to the Caspian Sea and India, where his successes gained for him the title of "the Great".

When Ptolemy IV died in 203 B.C., leaving an infant son, Antiochus III joined with Philip V of Macedon in an unsuccessful attempt to partition Egypt. But in 198 B.C. he won a decisive victory over the Egyptian forces led by Ptolemy V Epiphanes (203-181 B.C.). This gave Antiochus III military control over Judea—an unfortunate turn of events for Palestinian Jewry, as it was to lead to fiercer persecution than had ever before been experienced. The final years of Antiochus III were spent in campaigns in Asia Minor and in engagements with the Roman forces, who had now become prominent in the Mediterranean area.

The Roman empire came into being as the result of a prolonged process of development, the origins of which are far from certain. Excavations on the right bank of the Tiber have indicated the presence of certain Stone Age settlements, and there can be little doubt that migrating Indo-Europeans were in the general area of the Alban Hills at the end of the second millennium B.C.[5] In the early part of the first millennium B.C., they spread across the Latin Plain as far as the Palatine Hill on the Tiber, a movement which was coincident with that of the Sabine people who were moving from the central mountains into Latium. By the seventh century B.C., there were flourishing settlements of these immigrants in the region of the Palatine, the Esquiline and the Quirinal hills, following the same pattern of political and social organization and linked together by linguistic similarities. The religion of these peoples was primitive, being based upon a calendar of agricultural observances which antedated the arrival of the Etruscans.[6]

The growth of city-states in the eighth century B.C.

PLATE 11. Bronze Coins from the period of Herod Agrippa I.
(*By courtesy of the Trustees of the British Museum.*)

PLATE 12. A Greek Inscription from Thessalonica, naming Politarchs and other Civic Officials.
(By courtesy of the Trustees of the British Museum.)

may well have included the unifying of several small villages at Rome to form the state traditionally established by Romulus and Remus in 753 B.C., even though the legends relating to that occurrence as preserved by Livy and Dionysius of Halicarnassus need not be taken at all seriously. The power of the city-state of Rome was extended from the latter half of the sixth century B.C. when the Etruscan kings gained control over such Latin towns as Satricum, Praeneste and Ardea.

These invaders occupied the rich valley of the River Po, crushing the Umbrians who lived there and overrunning Etruria as far south as the Tiber. With characteristic energy, they developed farming by improving upon existing methods of agriculture, exploited the copper and iron mines of Etruria, and established a flourishing metal industry which attracted the attention of Phoenician and Greek traders. The Etruscan house of the Tarquins brought great commercial prosperity to Rome, which in the sixth century B.C. was already becoming as notable for its public buildings as for its material and political influence.[7]

Under Tarquin the Proud a revolt took place against the Etruscan usurpers, and after 508 B.C. a republican form of government, headed by two magistrates who were elected annually, was responsible for the administration of affairs in Rome. The Tarquins endeavoured to regain control of the city during the next decade, but suffered a decisive defeat at Lake Regillus in 499 B.C. Rome was also at war with the Latin cities at this time, and her conflict with the Etruscans compelled her to join a league of Latin towns including Ardea, Tusculum, Tibur, Aricia and Cora.

For the next two centuries, Rome was torn by class struggles between the older aristocracy, or patricians, and the rest of the population, the plebeians. But during the fifth century B.C., despite internal dissension, the

F

Republic attempted to reconquer those parts of Latium which had drifted away from Latin connections during the Etruscan wars. In the meantime, plebeian influence was growing steadily in Rome, and in 356 B.C. the first plebeian was made dictator. By 300 B.C. even the sacred colleges of the pontiffs and augurs, the traditional strongholds of patrician supremacy, had been opened to the plebeians and, when the legislative independence of the plebeian assembly was secured by about 285 B.C., the class struggle in Rome came to an end, at least for some time.

Serious though the internal pressures had been in the fifth century B.C., the Roman Republic had nevertheless embarked upon a fruitful programme of political con- solidation and conquest from 449 B.C. Southern Etruria was invaded and subjugated, the success of the campaign being aided greatly by attacks upon the Etruscans from Greek, Celtic and Samnite sources. Progress was halted for a time when the Gauls unexpectedly sacked Rome in 390 B.C. before withdrawing mysteriously from central Italy; but, with the conquest of the Aequi and Volsci in 343 B.C. and the campaigns against the Samnites in 341 B.C., the Romans had established themselves as the dominant power in central and southern Italy.

A second Samnite war broke out in 316 B.C., but the conflict was halted for six years in 304 B.C. by a revival of an ancient treaty with Rome. Hostilities were renewed in 298 B.C. when the Samnites allied with the Celts and the free tribes of Umbria against Rome. An Etruscan attack upon the Roman armies was repulsed, and after a lengthy struggle the Samnites were compelled to conclude a peace in 290 B.C.

Less than a decade later, the claims of Rome to supremacy in southern Italy were challenged by Pyrrhus, king of Epirus, who furnished aid to the city of Tarentum in its conflict with Rome.[8] In 280 B.C. Pyrrhus defeated the forces of the Republic in a battle at the River Liris, during which his elephants struck terror into the Roman soldiery. But Pyrrhus was more interested in occupying Sicily and North Africa than in conquering Rome, and after an abortive campaign in Sicily in 277 B.C. he returned to Italy, only to be defeated at Beneventum in 275 B.C.

He withdrew his shattered forces to Greece, and within the next decade Rome had become the undisputed master of Italy. This rule, however, was not so much that of absolute dominion over conquered subjects as the establishing of a confederacy under the guidance and protection of Rome. As was the case in ancient Greece, internal dissensions, feuds and differences of language made for considerable disunity in the land, and it was the task of Rome to unify her conquered territory by ensuring the loyalty of each part of the country to herself.

Once Rome had consolidated her position in Italy, she felt sufficiently prepared for the struggle with the successors of Alexander the Great for world dominance, although she had previously been inactive in the larger sphere of Mediterranean affairs. The Phoenician republic of Carthage in North Africa was now at the height of its development and presented a serious threat of absolute dominion over the Mediterranean. The situation became acute in 264 B.C. when the Carthaginians occupied part of Sicily in response to an appeal for help by the citadel of Messana against the king of Syracuse.

The First Punic War began in 265 B.C. with a Roman attack upon Messana, an event which witnessed the withdrawal of the Carthaginians and Syracusans. The struggle was to drag on until 241 B.C., however, when the Carthaginians under Hamilcar were completely defeated in a naval battle. Carthage then turned her attention to Spain, which she occupied between 237 and 219 B.C., and in 218 B.C. the Carthaginians under Hannibal crossed the Alps in order to invade Italy. This act precipitated the Second Punic War (218-201 B.C.), in which initial defeats were suffered by the Roman forces at the Ticinus and the Trebia. In 217 B.C. Hannibal inflicted a serious blow upon the Romans at Lake Trasimene and moved to within a few days' march of Rome.

The following year a Roman army was wiped out at Cannae and southern Italy rallied to the support of Hannibal. In 215 B.C. Philip V of Macedon concluded an alliance with the Carthaginian leader and threatened to invade Italy. Roman misfortunes were further heightened by the revolt of Syracuse in 214 B.C. and by the loss of the Greek cities on the south coast of Sicily in 212 B.C. But the Romans regrouped their forces, formed an alliance of Greek cities against Philip of Macedon and recaptured Syracuse in 212 B.C. The Carthaginians under Hasdrubal were defeated at the Metaurus in 207 B.C., and were finally expelled from Spain in the following year under Scipio. This talented soldier then crossed over to Africa in 204 B.C. and three years later defeated Hannibal at Zama, thus breaking the power of Carthage in the Mediterranean. A brief resurgence of military activity occurred when the city of Carthage was attacked by the king of Numidia in 151 B.C., and an anti-Carthaginian party in the Roman Senate demanded the total destruction of the city. This was achieved in 146 B.C.

In the meantime, Rome had become involved in aiding Pergamum against the Macedonians, who had formerly been allies of the Carthaginians, and the First Macedonian War in 214 B.C. brought the Roman forces into conflict with Philip of Macedon. The latter joined Antiochus III of Syria in 203 B.C. in an attempt to partition Egypt, but a threatened invasion from Pergamum, an ally of Rome, thwarted the larger plan. The

Second Macedonian War (200-197 B.C.) against Philip began with the landing of Roman legions in Epirus, and within three years the modest resistance offered by the Greeks had been crushed. Greece became a Roman dependency, and while Philip was still allowed to occupy the office of king he was stripped of all his former powers.

The feelings of enthusiasm for Rome which were evident when Greece was liberated soon turned to dissatisfaction and Rome was compelled to wage a Third Macedonian War (171-168 B.C.), which resulted in the complete extinction of the kingdom once ruled over by Philip. Indifferent Roman administration of Macedonia led to internal unrest, and finally in 146 B.C. it was constituted as a province under the control of a Roman magistrate.

The Syrian regime suffered a serious blow when Antiochus III became involved with Rome in Asia Minor and was defeated by Scipio Asiaticus at the Battle of Magnesia in 190 B.C. His death occurred in 187 B.C. as the result of a rebellion, and he was succeeded by Seleucus IV Philopator (187-175 B.C.), a weak ruler who relied heavily upon Rome for help. Imperial influence in the Near East was increased in 168 B.C. when the Egyptians under Ptolemy VI Philometor (180-146 B.C.) formally acknowledged the suzerainty of Rome.[9]

In Palestine, Antiochus IV Epiphanes (175-164 B.C.), who had been a hostage in Rome for fourteen years after the Battle of Magnesia, embarked upon a policy of Hellenization which brought him into immediate conflict with the Jews. He also launched a military campaign against Egypt in 168 B.C. and was within sight of Alexandria when his schemes were blocked by peremptory order of the Roman Senate. In reprisal, he attacked Jerusalem, profaned the Temple and burned the sacred books of the Law, an act which was followed in 167 B.C. by further restrictive measures against the Jewish religion.

Those Jews who were loyal to the ancient Mosaic traditions resisted all attempts to induce them to become pagan and a revolt broke out under the leadership of a Hasmonean named Mattathias. This was continued under Judas Maccabeus in 167 B.C. in what became known as the Maccabean Revolt. Antiochus IV died in 164 B.C. and was succeeded by his young son Antiochus V Eupator, who reigned for two years. During the first year of his rule, Judas Maccabeus launched an attack upon Jerusalem, which housed the forces of the Syrian governor Lysias. Although he was defeated, he was still able to conclude a peace with Lysias because the latter's position in Antioch had been suddenly imperilled by a revolt.

Trouble flared up again in the second year of the rule of Demetrius I (162-150 B.C.), the successor of Antiochus V, when a Syrian force was defeated by the Hasmoneans near Beth-horon in 161 B.C. However, the arrival of powerful reinforcements surprised the victorious Jews and in the ensuing conflict Judas Maccabeus was killed. According to Jewish historical sources,[10] Judas had tried to secure the protection of Rome, but orders from the Senate to Demetrius instructing him not to oppress the confederates of the Republic arrived too late to prevent Judas from being killed. Jonathan, brother of Judas Maccabeus, succeeded as military governor of Judea in 153 B.C. and became so influential that Demetrius ultimately sought his friendship. This policy was continued in the reign of Demetrius II (146-139 B.C.), who confirmed Jonathan in his position as high priest of the Jewish nation in 145 B.C.

The Syrian garrison withdrew from Jerusalem in 142 B.C. and, with its departure, the triumph of the Hasmoneans was complete. Judea became an independent state under the rule of an hereditary high priest, who initially also acted as civil governor. The independence of the nation was challenged in 134 B.C. by a new Syrian king, Antiochus VII Sidetes (139-129 B.C.), who demanded tribute from Judea. When this was ignored, Sidetes besieged Jerusalem and compelled John Hyrcanus (135-105 B.C.), the last surviving son of Simon Maccabeus, to become tributary to the Seleucid regime.

Hyrcanus repudiated this agreement in 129 B.C. after Antiochus VII had been killed in an expedition against the Parthians, and capitalized on the internal weaknesses of the Syrian kingdom to extend his own territories across the Jordan. His death in 105 B.C. was followed by the short reigns of his three sons, Aristobulus, Antigonus and Alexander Jannaeus. The last of these, who ruled from 104 to 78 B.C., was a weak and dissolute individual. He came into increasing conflict with the Pharisaic party in Judea and towards the end of his reign subjected them to severe persecution. This situation was redressed from 78 B.C. under the rule of his widow, Queen Alexandra, and from that time on the Pharisees were the dominant political group in Judea.

Because Rome was exerting greater influence than previously in Near Eastern political affairs in the second century B.C., it became increasingly impossible for the Roman population, and especially the nobility, to maintain their traditional forms of life in isolation from their geographic neighbours. The impact of Hellenic culture began to present a threat to the established order of things and, despite the warnings of Cato about the dangers of extravagance and luxury, a change of attitude towards the old ideals became clearly noticeable. Roman society manifested an increasingly unrepublican character, and matters came to a head in the form of a social revolution in the time of the Gracchi (133-121 B.C.).

Tiberius and Gaius Gracchus led the first systematic attack upon the senatorial government to which Rome had been subjected for a century and a half. In doing this they were, in effect, asserting the independence of the assembly and demonstrating the right of the people as such to exercise government. Economic distress provided the immediate occasion for the proposed reforms of the Gracchi, which were largely agrarian in nature. While Rome had been extending her influence in the eastern Mediterranean, the nobles and merchants were amassing huge fortunes at the expense of the small landholders, most of whom were faced with financial ruin due partly to the method of allotting conquered lands.[11]

Tiberius Gracchus proposed that the State should regain control of such common land as was not occupied by authorized persons and that restrictions should be imposed upon the amount of land under tenure in other cases. Although this general objective was also pursued by Gaius Gracchus and extended to the colonies which he founded in southern Italy in order to implement the reforms of his brother, the agrarian programme of the Gracchi had little lasting effect. The class struggle between patricians and plebeians flared up again, although the sovereignty of the people was being recognized as a much more virile concept than it had been previously.

Ten years after Gaius died the supremacy of the Senate was again challenged on the matter of foreign administration. The situation came to a head when Jugurtha usurped control of Numidia and defied the authority of the Romans. Marius (118-86 B.C.), a talented plebeian, led the forces which crushed the revolt, and shortly afterwards was elected consul. In 102 and 101 B.C. he defeated the armies of the Cimbri and Teutones which had threatened to invade Rome, and in consequence of this his position as a popular dictator became secure. Marius instituted certain military reforms which increased the fighting efficiency of the Roman legions and made the army a much more democratic organization.

The agrarian and administrative reforms suggested by Drusus in 91 B.C. served only to fan the flames of class discontent, and his assassination that same year was followed by riots in central and southern Italy. Marius and his rival legate Sulla restored a degree of order in the north, but it was only when the various communities in Italy were offered the Roman franchise in 90 B.C. that the insurgents ceased their attacks. A conservative re-action occurred with the dictatorship of Sulla (88-78 B.C.), who was given unprecedented powers to enact laws and reorganize the Roman constitution. Unfortunately, Sulla was not equal to these responsibilities, and he left behind a legacy of hatred and suspicion which obscured many of his more useful administrative reforms, particularly those which resulted in the laying of a foundation for Roman criminal law.

The regime of Sulla lasted until 78 B.C., when it was overthrown by Pompey, a former officer under Sulla. In 75 B.C. this man had been sent by the Senate to quell a revolt by a Roman governor in Spain, and had returned victorious in 71 B.C. only to discover that the revolt of the Thracian slave Spartacus in Italy herself two years earlier had come within measurable distance of success. The degree of unrest which had contributed so much to the cause of Spartacus showed that the conflict between the various levels of society in Italy was far from over. Pompey was hailed as the one person who could remedy the system imposed by Sulla, and accordingly he was elected consul in 70 B.C.

The orator and consul Cicero cherished the hope that some sort of moderate central party could be formed which would make unnecessary the incessant conflicts between the various Roman generals and the Senate. But Pompey was indifferent to the traditional politics of the Republic, and Cicero's pleas fell largely upon deaf ears. When his consulship ended, Pompey remained

aloof from affairs in Rome until 67 B.C., when he left
the city to wage war against Cilician pirates who were
threatening the maritime trade of the entire Mediterranean area.

After 67 B.C. the dominant figures in Rome were
Cicero and Julius Caesar (101-44 B.C.). The former advo-
cated that the old constitution be maintained, with the
Senate as the supreme governing body and appointed
freely from the citizenry without regard to wealth or
position. The influence of Cicero increased when in 63
B.C. he quelled an attempt by Cataline to usurp the
government and his political fortunes were at their height
when Pompey returned in triumph, having crushed the
Cilician pirates. In addition, Pompey had marched
along the Upper Euphrates region as far as the Caspian
Sea and had deposed Antiochus XIII, the last king of
the Seleucid Dynasty, thus making Syria and Palestine
a Roman province.

In 60 B.C. a triumvirate consisting of Pompey, Caesar
and Crassus was formed to govern Rome, and the following year Caesar obtained the military command of Gaul.
Crassus was killed by the Parthians at Carrhae in 53
B.C., and from that time onwards there arose increasing
hostility between Pompey and Caesar. Despite various
efforts at compromise, the Senate recalled Caesar in
49 B.C., who replied to this challenge to his authority by
crossing the Rubicon and invading Italy. A series of civil
wars broke out in the empire, including Spain, where the
supporters of Pompey were quickly suppressed, and
Macedonia, where Pompey was killed at the Battle of
Pharsalus in 48 B.C. Unrest in Egypt prompted Caesar
to set out for Alexandria, where on his arrival he demanded that King Ptolemy and his sister Cleopatra
should submit to his rule.

In 46 B.C. Caesar was made dictator for a decade, and
he set about establishing his veterans in Italy and else-

where by founding colonies. However, he was unable to control the state of near anarchy caused by the conflict of the various classes in Roman society, and his assumption of regal status in 44 B.C. precipitated his death at the hands of dissident senators led by Marcus Brutus. Political power then passed into the hands of Octavius, Lepidus and Mark Antony, three former lieutenants of Julius Caesar.

This triumvirate defeated Brutus and Cassius, who had become masters of Syria and Asia Minor, at Philippi in 42 B.C. While Octavius was consolidating his position as head of the Roman State, Antony was living riotously in the East, where he met Cleopatra, and on his return to Italy in 40 B.C. a conflict between himself and Octavius appeared inevitable. Relations between the two men were smoothed over, however, and personal antagonisms were set aside in the face of revolts in Sicily, Asia Minor and Syria.

The rupture between Antony and Octavius finally took place in 33 B.C. when, with Antony's apparent support, the natural son of Julius Caesar and Cleopatra was put forward as the true heir of Caesar and the opponent of Octavius. Octavius declared war on Cleopatra in 32 B.C., and prepared to attack the fleet commanded by Antony as it lay in its winter quarters in the Bay of Prevesa. A great naval battle took place at Actium in 31 B.C., which resulted in the defeat of the forces of Antony and Cleopatra.

Later that same year Cleopatra opened negotiations with Octavius, but when the latter finally marched on Alexandria in 30 B.C. she and her lover committed suicide. Egypt was formally annexed as a Roman province, and Octavius was hailed on all sides as the man who had re-established the sovereignty of Rome throughout the civilized world. Among the many other privileges accorded him, Octavius was given the right in

27 B.C. by the Roman Senate to assume the cognomen of
"Augustus".

In his attempts to bring stability to the empire, Augustus restored the operations of civil government to the
Senate, while at the same time retaining control over the
army and foreign affairs. The Senate governed those
provinces which did not need to be guarded by Roman
legions, while Augustus himself was given proconsular
authority over the others. So remarkable were his gifts
of organization that, within a few years, he had become
renowned for bringing peace and prosperity to the
inhabited world. During his long life (63 B.C.-A.D.14),
the *pax Romana* became a reality for a great many areas
of his scattered empire, establishing procedures which
were to be followed for the succeeding three centuries.
Seldom, if ever, had a ruler been so venerated by his
subjects, and only the Babe of Bethlehem, born under his
rule about 4 B.C., was destined to claim a wider allegiance
in the world.

APPENDIX

The foregoing outline of ancient Near Eastern history may have given the reader the general impression that it is possible to think in terms of a settled chronology for the peoples and times under examination. While the results of historical and archaeological research have made certain dates assured, particularly where the Greek and Roman empires are concerned, there are other periods for which no certain information concerning specific dates is yet available.

Despite all that is now known about the ancient Near East, there are still insufficient primary source materials to draw up a coherent chronological system to which the various cultures can be related with complete confidence in all points of detail. A further aspect of the problem lies in the fact that some of the necessary information which is already available to scholars is amenable to different kinds of interpretation, and this unfortunate state of affairs gives undue place to the purely subjective element in scholarly evaluations.

However, certain fixed points have been established for Babylonian and Assyrian chronology on the one hand, and for Egyptian dating-sequences on the other. As a result, it has become possible to employ these as "vertical" lines and to establish certain "horizontal" synchronisms so as to form a reasonably assured grid-system upon which the chronologies of the Near Eastern peoples can be imposed.

It has, nevertheless, to be realized that the chronologies of both Babylonia and Egypt are themselves far from complete in all aspects, and that in each case there is a "high" and a "low" chronology for certain periods. This situation, which is as unfortunate for the historian as it is embarrassing for the Near Eastern scholar, has resulted largely from varying interpretations of the same archaeological or historical evidence.

Thus the "high" chronology of the First Babylonian Dynasty assigned Hammurabi of Babylon to a period as early as 2123-2081 B.C., due in part to the identification of Hammurabi with Amraphel, king of Shinar, who was mentioned in Genesis 14: 1 seq.[1] In 1928 the First Dynasty was placed in the period of 2067-2025 B.C.,[2] then reduced by Thureau-Dangin by more than half a century to c. 2003-1961 B.C.[3] and still further by Pirot to c. 1947-1905 B.C.[4]

The "low" chronology resulted from the discovery that Hammurabi was actually a junior contemporary of Shamshi-Adad I.[5] In 1928 Albright[6] revised his earlier dating and suggested an accession-year of about 1870 B.C. for Hammurabi, and two years later reduced this figure to c. 1800-1760 B.C.[7] As a consequence of additional published Babylonian tablets, Albright reduced his dating of Hammurabi still further to 1728-1686 B.C.[8]

Even this date was regarded as being too high by certain scholars,[9] who preferred instead to follow an "ultra low" chronology which assigned a period of about 1704-1662 B.C. for the time of Hammurabi. Before these wide variations are shrugged off as being characteristic of the activities of experts, it must be remembered that there are a great many technical issues involved in these considerations which demand an advanced degree of competence for their solution.

Although the chronological picture with regard to ancient Egypt is a little more stable than its Babylonian counterpart, it too has been revised considerably. No small degree of confusion is occasioned for the historian by the fact that Egyptologists have been unable to agree upon a precise chronology for ancient Egypt prior to the Saitic revival (663-525 B.C.). Egyptian historical sources include king-lists and annals from various periods, but a degree of caution must always be entertained in approaching descriptive or annalistic material from the Egyptian past, since it is frequently not so much factual history as propaganda, presenting a "correct" view of events for the benefit of future generations.

The grouping of Egyptian rulers into dynasties was actually the work of Manetho, an Egyptian priest who lived in the third century B.C. Using extant historical sources, he compiled a history of his country in which he listed the pharaohs in terms of thirty dynasties (subsequently extended to thirty-one), a classification which scholars have found to be so convenient that it has been perpetuated in modern times. The rulers of the first two dynasties were listed on small ivory tablets, while the celebrated Palermo Stone, dated about 2400 B.C.,[10] furnished an account of events associated with the first six dynasties in the form of annals.

Even here, however, there are problems connected with the dating of the First and Second Dynasties, and these have led to a "high" and a "low" chronology for the period. The former was generally favoured by earlier scholars, the most notable of whom were Champollion, who dated the First Dynasty about 5867 B.C., and Petrie, who dated it in 4777 B.C. J. H. Breasted, however, reduced this latter by over 1,300 years,[11] but even as late as 1956 J. A. Wilson was dating the beginning of the First Dynasty about 3100 B.C.[12]

The "low" chronology derived its name from the synchronisms and agreements with a comparatively low dating for the First Dynasty of Babylon. Scholars who favour this approach have assigned the First and Second Dynasties of Egypt to the proto-dynastic period, about 2900-2760 B.C.[13]

Again there are certain problems connected with the chronology of the Eighteenth Dynasty, which introduced the New Kingdom period (c. 1570-1150 B.C.). These particular difficulties concern the periods of time spanned by the reign of Amenophis II, the assumed co-regency of Amenophis III and Akhenaten (Amenophis IV), the reigns of Tutankhamun, Haremhab and Seti I respectively, and the date when Ramses II came to the throne.[14]

Nevertheless, as has already been remarked, there are certain dates in Near Eastern chronology which can be regarded as firmly fixed. The fall of Samaria in 722/1 B.C. is certified by reference to the annals of Sargon of Assyria. Again, the first assault upon Jerusalem by the Babylonians occurred on 15th/16th March 597 B.C., as is now known from contemporary cuneiform records.

These and other "fixed points" form the basis of a chronological pattern to which other less certain data can be related. As further archaeological and historical researches bring to light other assured dates in Near Eastern history, it will become increasingly possible to formulate a reliable chronology of the principal events which occurred in the ancient world.

NOTES TO CHAPTERS

Chapter 1

1. J. Manchip White, *Teach Yourself Anthropology* (1960), p. 28.
2. On this general subject *vide* R. Broom, *Natural History* (1925), XXV, p. 409 seq.; L. Leakey, *Adam's Ancestors* (1934), p. 207 seq.; W. E. Le Gros Clark, *Nature* (1948), CLXI, p. 667 seq.; G. H. R. Von Koenigswald, *Meeting Prehistoric Man* (1956), p. 151 seq., *et al.*
3. *Vide* H. J. Movius, *Papers of the Peabody Museum* (1944), XIX, No. 3, p. 82; F. Weidenreich, *Apes, Giants and Man* (1946), p. 60 seq.; E. A. Hooton, *Up from the Ape* (1946), p. 350 seq.; W. E. Le Gros Clark, *The Fossil Evidence for Human Evolution* (1955), p. 81 seq.; A. Montagu, *Man: His First Million Years* (1958), p. 44 seq., *et al.*
4. W. F. Albright, *The Archaeology of Palestine* (1949), p. 55 f.
5. R. J. Braidwood, *Antiquity* (1950), XXIV, p. 190 seq.; cf. *American Journal of Archaeology* (1949), LIII, p. 50 f.; V. G. Childe, *New Light From the Most Ancient East* (1953 ed.), p. 104 f.
6. K. M. Kenyon, *Palestine Exploration Quarterly* (1952), LXXXIV, p. 62 seq.; *ibid.* (1953), LXXXV, p. 81 seq.; *id.* (1954), LXXXVI, p. 45 seq.; *id.* (1955), LXXXVII, p. 106 seq.; *id.* (1956), LXXXVIII, p. 67 seq.; *id.* (1957), LXXXIX, p. 101 seq.; K. M.

Kenyon, *Digging Up Jericho* (1957); *ibid.*, *The Biblical Archaeologist* (1953), XVI, No. 3, p. 46; *id.* (1954), XVII, No. 4, p. 98 seq.

7. Cf. R. J. Braidwood, *The Near East and the Foundations of Civilization* (1952), p. 23 seq.

8. W. F. Albright, *From the Stone Age to Christianity* (1957 ed.), p. 134.

9. Sir M. Wheeler, *Antiquity* (1956), CXIX, p. 132 seq.

10. W. A. Fairservis, *The Origins of Oriental Civilization* (1959), p. 11.

11. Cf. H. Breuil, *Archives de l'Institut de Paleontologie Humaine* (1928), Mem. 4, p. 120 f.

12. On the characteristics of these peoples *vide* C. S. Coon, S. M. Garn and J. B. Birdsell, *Races* (1950), p. 130 f.

13. E. A. Hooton, *Up from the Ape*, p. 402.

14. Cf. E. C. Worman, *Journal of the Washington Academy of Sciences* (1949), XXXIX, No. 6, p. 181 seq.

15. W. A. Fairservis, *Anthropological Papers of the American Museum of Natural History* (1956), XLV, II, p. 356.

16. For Neolithic sites in Red China discovered subsequent to 1949 *vide* H. Nai, *Archaeology* (1957), X, No. 3, p. 181 seq.

17. J. Finegan, *Light From the Ancient Past* (1946), p. 15 and plate 1.

18. V. G. Childe, *New Light From the Most Ancient East*, p. 113 seq.

19. E. A. Speiser, *Bulletin of the American Schools of Oriental Research* (1937), No. 66, p. 2 seq.

20. The Erech of Genesis 10: 10.

21. M. Von Oppenheim, *Der Tell Halaf* (1931), p. 199 seq.

22. V. G. Childe, *New Light From the Most Ancient East*, p. 33 f.

23. V. G. Childe, *New Light From the Most Ancient East*, p. 57 f.

Chapter 2

1. S. N. Kramer, *History Begins at Sumer* (1958), pp. 57 seq., 230 ff.

2. H. Frankfort, *The Birth of Civilization in the Near East* (1956), p. 67.

3. H. Frankfort, *Kingship and the Gods* (1948), p. 237 f.

4. C. L. Woolley, *Ur of the Chaldees* (1950), p. 74 seq.

5. For the Gilgamesh Epic *vide Ancient Near Eastern Texts Relating to the Old Testament* (1950), p. 72 seq.

6. On the achievements of the Sumerians *vide* C. L. Woolley, *The Sumerians* (1928); *ibid., The Royal Cemetery: Ur Excavations* (1934), II; A. Falkenstein, *Journal of World History* (1954), I, p. 784 seq.; H. Frankfort, *The Art and Architecture of the Ancient Orient* (1955), p. 1 seq. and plates 1-69; R. J. Forbes, *Studies in Ancient Technology* (1955-56), I-IV; S. N. Kramer, *From the Tablets of Sumer* (1956); O. Neugebauer, *The Exact Sciences in Antiquity* (1957).

7. J. Finegan, *Light From the Ancient Past*, plate 17.

8. C. L. Woolley, *Ur of the Chaldees*, p. 89 seq. and plate 9 (a).

9. C. L. Woolley, *The Sumerians*, p. 169.

10. J. Finegan, *Light from the Ancient Past*, plate 22. This monument is now in the Louvre in Paris.

11. *Ancient Near Eastern Texts Relating to the Old Testament*, p. 164 seq.

12. O. Neugebauer, *Mathematische Keilschrift-Texte* (1935-37), I-III; *ibid., The Exact Sciences in Antiquity* (1957).

13. *Ancient Near Eastern Texts Relating to the Old Testament*, p. 60 seq.

14. *Ancient Near Eastern Texts Relating to the Old Testament*, p. 72 seq.

15. Cf. A. Heidel, *The Gilgamesh Epic and Old Testament Parallels* (1949), p. 4 seq.

16. Cf. O. R. Gurney, *The Hittites* (1952), p. 18 seq.

17. O. R. Gurney, *The Hittites*, p. 95.

18. On the Hittites *vide* J. Garstang, *The Hittite Empire* (1930); A. Goetze, *Hethiter, Churriter und Assyrer* (1936); D. G. Hogarth, *The Cambridge Ancient History* (1926), II, ix; R. Naumann, *Die Hethiter* (1948); F. F. Bruce, *The Hittites and the Old Testament* (1948); E. Neufeld, *The Hittite Laws* (1952); S. Lloyd, *Early Anatolia* (1956); A. Goetze, *Kleinasien* (1958 ed.), *et al.*

19. Cf. E. Chiera, *They Wrote on Clay* (1938); C. H. Gordon, *Introduction to Old Testament Times* (1953), p. 100 seq.; R. K. Harrison, *Archaeology of the Old Testament* (1962), p. 24 seq.

20. On the Horites and their culture *vide* E. A. Speiser, *Annual of the American Schools of Oriental Research* (1933), XIII, p. 13 seq.; A. Goetze, *Hethiter, Churriter und Assyrer* (1936); W. F. Albright, *Bulletin of the American Schools of Oriental Research* (1942), No. 94, p. 12 seq.; I. J. Gelb, *Hurrians and Subarians* (1944); B. Landsberger, *Journal of Cuneiform Studies* (1954), LVIII, p. 59.

21. On the Habiru *vide* J. Bottéro, *Cahiers de la Société asiatique* (1954), XII; M. Greenberg, *The Hab/piru* (1955).

22. M. S. Vats, *Excavations at Harappā* (1940), I, p. 470 seq.; on Mohenjo-daro archaeology *vide* E. J. H. Mackay, *Further Excavations at Mohenjo-daro* (1938), I, p. 4 *passim*; J. Marshall, *Mohenjo-daro and the Indus Civilization* (1931), I, p. 2 *passim*.

23. For attempts at chronological evaluation of these artefacts *vide* L. Ward in R. W. Erich (Ed.), *Relative Chronologies in Old World Archaeology* (1954), p. 137 f.

Chapter 3
1. Genesis 10: 22 f.
2. Genesis 22: 20 f.
3. O. R. Gurney, *The Hittites*, p. 29 f.

4. I. E. S. Edwards, *The Pyramids of Egypt* (1947), p. 86 seq.

5. G. Steindorff and K. C. Seele, *When Egypt Ruled the East* (1963), p. 124.

6. R. M. Engberg, *The Hyksos Reconsidered* (1939), p. 4 seq.; H. Stock, *Studien zur Geschichte und Archäologie der 13 bis 17 Dynastie Ägyptens* (1942), p. 19 seq.; T. Säve-Söderberg, *Journal of Egyptian Archaeology* (1951), XXXVII, p. 53 seq.; J. van Seters, *The Hyksos* (1966), p. 9 seq.

7. C. H. Gordon, *Introduction to Old Testament Times*, p. 58 f.

8. J. A. Wilson, *The Culture of Ancient Egypt* (1956), p. 179 seq.

9. J. Finegan, *Light From the Ancient Past*, p. 40.

10. J. A. Knudtzon, *Die El-Amarna Tafeln* (1907-15); S. A. B. Mercer, *The Tell el-Amarna Tablets* (1939); W. F. Albright in *Ancient Near Eastern Texts Relating to the Old Testament*, p. 488 f.

11. J. Finegan, *Light From the Ancient Past*, p. 97.

12. O. R. Gurney, *The Hittites*, p. 39.

13. R. K. Harrison, *A History of Old Testament Times* (1957), p. 92.

14. Cf. Exodus 1: 11.

15. G. E. Wright and F. V. Filson, *The Westminster Historical Atlas to the Bible* (1945), p. 37.

16. S. L. Caiger, *Bible and Spade* (1936), p. 111 f. Cf. *Ancient Near Eastern Texts Relating to the Old Testament*, p. 378.

17. J. Finegan, *Light From the Ancient Past*, p. 108 f.

Chapter 4

1. Cf. R. A. S. Macalister, *The Philistines, Their History and Civilization* (1914); W. F. Albright, *Annual of the American Schools of Oriental Research* (1932), XII, p. 53 seq.; A. Furumark, *The Chronology of Mycenaean*

Pottery (1941), p. 118 seq.; V. Georgiev, *Jahrbuch für Kleinasiatische Forschung* (1950), I, p. 136 seq.; C. H. Gordon, *Antiquity* (1956), XXX, p. 22 seq.; K. M. Kenyon, *Archaeology in the Holy Land* (1960), p. 221 seq.

2. Genesis, chapters 37-50.

3. Cf. H. M. Orlinsky, *Ancient Israel* (1954), p. 33.

4. Exodus 1: 8 seq.

5. Cf. K. A. Kitchen, *Ancient Orient and Old Testament* (1966), pp. 156 ff.; *ibid., New Bible Dictionary* (1962), p. 343 f.

6. Cf. G. E. Wright, *An Introduction to Biblical Archaeology* (1960), p. 48 seq.; R. K. Harrison, *Archaeology of the Old Testament* (1963), p. 49 seq.

7. *Ancient Near Eastern Texts Relating to the Old Testament*, p. 25 seq.

8. Cf. 1 Kings 9: 15 seq.

9. Cf. N. Glueck, *The Other Side of the Jordan* (1940), p. 50 seq.

10. 1 Kings 15: 18.

11. 2 Samuel 8: 5 f.

12. 1 Kings 20: 34.

13. J. Finegan, *Light From the Ancient Past*, p. 171 f.

14. 2 Kings 17: 4.

15. 2 Kings 19: 32 seq.

16. Jeremiah 22: 18.

17. D. J. Wiseman, *Chronicles of Chaldean Kings (626-556 B.C.) in the British Museum* (1956).

Chapter 5

1. Cf. J. M. Todd, *The Ancient World* (1938), p. 81 seq.

2. C. H. Gordon, *Before the Bible* (1962), p. 19.

3. S. N. Marinatos, *Studies Presented to David Moore Robinson*, p. 126.

4. For a general survey of the archaeology *vide* J. D. S. Pendlebury, *The Archaeology of Crete* (1939).

5. Cf. J. Chadwick, *The Decipherment of Linear B* (1958), p. 34 seq.

6. M. Ventris and J. Chadwick, *Documents in Mycenaean Greek* (1956).

7. On this subject *vide* A. Furumark, *Linear A und die alkretische Sprache* (1956); S. Davis, *Greece and Rome* (1959), VI, p. 20 seq.; J. Chadwick, *Antiquity* (1959), XXXIII, p. 269 seq.; W. C. Brice, *Inscriptions in the Minoan Script of Class A* (1961); C. H. Gordon, *Before the Bible*, p. 206 seq.

8. C. E. Robinson, *Hellas: A Short History of Ancient Greece* (1955), pp. 30 ff.

9. C. H. Gordon, *Introduction to Old Testament Times*, p. 89 seq.; *ibid.*, *Before the Bible*, p. 12 *passim*.

10. R. W. Rogers, *Cuneiform Parallels to the Old Testament* (1912), p. 383; *Ancient Near Eastern Texts Relating to the Old Testament*, p. 315.

11. Ezra 1: 2 seq., 6: 3 ff.

12. Cf. A. Cowley, *Aramaic Papyri of the Fifth Century B.C.* (1923); *Ancient Near Eastern Texts Relating to the Old Testament*, p. 222 f.

13. Cf. T. T. Rice, *The Scythians* (1957), p. 46 f.

14. J. B. Bury, *A History of Greece* (1931), p. 346 seq.

15. A. T. Olmstead, *History of the Persian Empire* (1948), p. 358 seq.

16. P. K. Hitti, *History of Syria* (1951), p. 231.

17. R. W. Rogers, *A History of Ancient Persia* (1929), p. 307.

Chapter 6

1. W. Tarn and G. T. Griffiths, *Hellenistic Civilisation* (1959 ed.), p. 295 seq.

2. M. Rostovtzeff, *The Cambridge Ancient History* (1928), VII, p. 109 seq.

3. Cf. S. Zeitlin, *History of the Second Jewish Commonwealth* (1933), p. 6 seq.

4. Cf. R. H. Pfeiffer, *History of New Testament Times* (1949), p. 179.

5. D. Randall-MacIver, *Villanovans and Early Etruscans* (1925), p. 10 seq.; H. Last, *The Cambridge Ancient History*, VII, p. 333 seq.

6. W. Warde Fowler, *The Religious Experience of the Roman People* (1911), p. 92.

7. H. Last, *The Cambridge Ancient History*, VII, p. 385 f.

8. T. Frank, *The Cambridge Ancient History*, VII, p. 641 seq.

9. Cf. V. A. Tcherikover and A. Fuks, *Corpus Papyrorum Judaicarum* (1957), I, p. 20 seq.

10. 1 Maccabees 8: 31.

11. H. Last, *The Cambridge Ancient History*, VII, p. 468 seq.

Appendix

1. So. W. F. Albright, *Revue d'Assyriologie* (1921), XVIII, p. 94; S. A. Cook, *Cambridge Ancient History* (1924), I, p. 154; L. W. King, *A History of Babylon from the Foundation of the Monarchy to the Persian Conquest* (1919), p. 106 seq.

2. S. H. Langdon and J. K. Fotheringham, *The Venus Tablets of Ammizaduga* (1928), p. 66 f.; cf. A. G. Shortt, *Journal of the British Astronomical Association* (1947), LVII, p. 208.

3. F. Thureau-Dangin, *Revue d'Assyriologie* (1927), XXIV, p. 181 seq.

4. L. Pirot, *Supplément au Dictionnaire de la Bible* (1928), I, col. 7 seq.

5. F. Thureau-Dangin, *Revue d'Assyriologie* (1937), XXXIV, p. 135 seq.

6. W. F. Albright, *Bulletin of the American Schools of Oriental Research* (1938), No. 69, p. 18 f.

7. W. F. Albright, *Bulletin of the American Schools of Oriental Research* (1940), No. 77, p. 25 f.

8. W. F. Albright, *Bulletin of the American Schools of Oriental Research* (1942), No. 88, p. 28 seq.; *ibid.* (1952), No. 126, pp. 24 ff.; *id.* (1956), No. 144, p. 26 seq.

9. F. M. Th. Böhl, *Mededeelingen der Koninklijke Nederlandsche Akademie van Wetenschappen* (1946), IX, No. 10, p. 341 seq.; K. Schubert, *Wiener Zeitschrift für die Kunde des Morgenlandes* (1948-52), LI, p. 21 seq.; E. Weidner, *Archiv für Orientforschung* (1945-51), XV, p. 85 seq.

10. For the stone *vide* J. Finegan, *Light From the Ancient Past*, plate 27; J. H. Breasted, *Ancient Records of Egypt* (1906-07), I, Sect. 76 seq.; *ibid.*, *Bulletin de l'Institut Français d'Archéologie Orientale* (1930-31), XXX, p. 709 seq.

11. J. H. Breasted, *The Conquest of Civilisation* (1938), p. 64 f.

12. J. A. Wilson, *The Culture of Ancient Egypt* (1956), p. 43; *ibid.*, *Interpreter's Dictionary of the Bible* (1962), II, p. 44.

13. Cf. P. van der Meer, *Orientalia Neerlandica* (1948), p. 23 seq.; W. F. Albright, *Bulletin of the American Schools of Oriental Research* (1950), No. 199, p. 29; A. Scharff and A. Moortgat, *Agypten und Vorderasien im Altertum* (1950), p. 25 seq.

14. For some solutions to the problem *vide* R. Engelbach, *Annales du Service des Antiquités de l'Égypte* (1940), XL, p. 133 seq.; M. B. Rowton, *Journal of Egyptian Archaeology* (1948), XXXIV, p. 57 seq.; K. Seele, *Journal of Near Eastern Studies* (1955), XIV, p. 168 seq.; R. A. Parker, *Journal of Near Eastern Studies* (1957), XVI, p. 39 seq.; W. F. Albright, *From the Stone Age to Christianity* (1957 ed.), p. 404 seq.

SELECT BIBLIOGRAPHY

(of works not mentioned previously)

Adams, R. M. *The Growth of Early Old World Civilizations*, 1965.

Astour, M. C. *Hellenosemitica*, 1965.

Baikie, J. *The Sea Kings of Crete*, 1926.

Botsford G. W. and Sihler, E. G. *Hellenic Civilization*, 1924.

Ceram, C. W. *The Secret of the Hittites*, 1956.

Ceram, C. W. *Narrow Pass Black Mountain*, 1956.

Gardiner, A. *Egypt of the Pharaohs*, 1961.

Glover, T. R. *The Ancient World*, 1935.

Gordon, C. H. *Ugarit and Minoan Crete*, 1967.

Grosvenor, M. B. (Ed.) *Everyday Life in Bible Times*, 1967.

Hamilton, E. *The Greek Way to Western Civilization*, 1958.

Herzfeld, E. *Archaeological History of Iran*, 1935.

Jones, A. H. M. *The Greek City from Alexander to Justinian*, 1951.

Kitto, H. D. F. *The Greeks*, 1951.

Lloyd, S. *The Art of the Ancient Near East*, 1961.

Mackay, E. *Early Indus Civilizations*, 1948.

Mertz, B. *Temples, Tombs and Hieroglyphs*, 1964.

Moscati, S. *Ancient Semitic Civilizations*, 1957.

Parrot, A. *Nineveh and Babylon*, 1961.

Payne, R. *The Splendor of Greece*, 1960.

Piggott, S. *Prehistoric India*, 1950.

Rostovtzeff, M. I. *A History of the Ancient World*, 1926.

Rostovtzeff, M. I. *Social and Economic History of the Hellenistic World*, 1941, 3 volumes.

Sauneron, S. *The Priests of Ancient Egypt*, 1960.

Thomson, G. *The Prehistoric Aegean*, 1949.

Watson, W. *Archaeology in China*, 1960.

Wheeler, Sir M. *Rome Beyond the Imperial Frontiers*, 1954.

Winlock, H. E. *The Rise and Fall of the Middle Kingdom in Thebes*, 1947.

Zimmern, A. E. *The Greek Commonwealth*, 1931.

INDEX